Coping with

D0103053

SELF-MUTILATION

A HELPING BOOK FOR TEENS WHO HURT THEMSELVES

Alicia Clarke, M.A.

THE ROSEN PUBLISHING GROUP, INC./NEW YORK

Published in 1999 by The Rosen Publishing Group, Inc.
29 East 21st Street, New York, NY 10010

Cover Photo by John Bentham

First Edition

Library of Congress Cataloging-in-Publication Data

Clarke, Alicia.
  Coping with self-mutilation : a helping book for teens who hurt them-selves / Alicia Clarke. — 1st ed.
      p. cm. — (coping with)
  Includes bibliographical references and index.
  Summary: Discusses self-mutilating behavior in teens, including possi-ble causes and avenues for recovery.
  ISBN 0-8239-2559-5
  1. Self-mutilation—Juvenile literature. [1. Self-mutilation.] I. Title. II. Series : Coping with series (New York, N.Y.)
  RJ506.S44 C58 1999
  615.85′82′00835—dc21
                                                                      98-54123
                                                                        CIP
                                                                         AC

Manufactured in the United States of America

About the Author

Alicia Clarke, M.A., is an outpatient therapist with Parkside Behavioral Health Services and Hospital of Tulsa, Oklahoma. She has practiced in the mental health field since 1974, working as a psychiatric aide in a state hospital, a clinical social worker in a private hospital as well as in mental health centers in Norman and Tulsa, and as a psychology instructor in Midwest City and Tulsa. She is currently cofacilitating a group for survivors of childhood sexual abuse.

Contents

Introduction

Sally is in the tenth grade. She comes from a middle class family; her father is a university professor and her mother is a computer programmer. Sally is friendly and popular. To her teachers, she is a normal, above-average student. Sally has long blond hair and flawless skin—except at her wrists. Usually she wears long sleeves to hide her wrists, which are crisscrossed with scars from daily cutting.

Sally doesn't tell anyone what she does at home when her parents argue. She doesn't tell because she doesn't think anyone would understand it, and she's afraid others would make her stop cutting. She's afraid other people will think she's crazy. But for Sally it's the only way she can calm herself. When her parents start to argue, Sally feels pain in her stomach, and she closes the door to her bedroom. Her parents get louder and threaten each other with divorce. Sally just wants all the noise and fighting to stop. She turns on her music, but it doesn't cover the sound. She tries to do her homework, but she can't concentrate. She just wants the stress to go away. The only thing that calms her down is to cut on her wrists.

She keeps a pocketknife in her desk drawer under some notebook paper. She slides the knife lightly over her skin, watching the faint red line that develops. Then she presses harder with the knife. Bright drops of blood seep out of the cut; she drags the knife again over the same cut. A steady trickle of blood oozes from the cut. Sally starts to feel calm and relaxed. She doesn't hear the screaming and yelling anymore. She watches the blood run down her wrist. In a moment or so, she'll have to wash the area clean, but for now she just wants to look at it. It will burn later. Right now though, it doesn't hurt at all.

Sally doesn't have a mental illness. She knows what she's doing and keeps her cutting a secret. She's not trying to commit suicide either. For Sally, cutting is a way to cope with all of the anxiety building up inside her. Cutting, though, only provides Sally with temporary relief. When she is done cutting, she still has to face her parents' constant fighting.

This is just one of the times Sally has cut herself. Self-mutilation usually happens again and again, escalating to dangerous levels. Eventually, some self-mutilating teens will learn healthier ways to handle their feelings. Other teens, however, can't stop and continue self-mutilation for many years. Either way, as long as someone is self-mutilating, there is a serious problem that needs to be addressed.

Self-mutilation is defined by Dr. Armando Favazza, a professor of psychiatry at the University of Missouri at Columbia medical school and author of *Bodies Under Siege*, the first book to explore self-mutilation, as "the direct, deliberate destruction or alteration of one's own body tissue without conscious suicidal intent." Psychologist Tracy Alderman, author of *The Scarred Soul*, defines self-mutilation as "self-inflicted violence." Doing violence to your own body encompasses more self-destructive behaviors than just those that actually "mutilate" your body.

Many doctors and mental health professionals were not fully aware of this problem until recently. In the past, it was often considered strictly a sign of borderline personality disorder or a sign of suicidal tendencies. Today, many doctors and psychologists have learned more about self-mutilating behaviors and are beginning to understand their causes. They now know that such actions are not usually suicide attempts. More often, some people use self mutilation as a way to handle overwhelming emotional pain and as an attempt to regain control over their bodies.

Because their behavior is out of control, people who self-mutilate usually need support to help them stop hurting themselves. Others—usually those who do less serious damage to themselves—can learn more positive ways to deal with stress on their own. Before you can determine the treatment, however, you have to understand the problem.

Self-mutilation is a hard topic to discuss. If you have a friend whom you think cuts herself, you may avoid talking to her about it because it's too uncomfortable. If you are self-mutilating, it can be difficult to talk to someone about your condition. Like Sally, you may be afraid that others will judge you and think you are crazy. But there is help available and people who understand how you're feeling. Reading this book is the first step to finding positive, healthy ways to deal with the emotional pain, anger, hurt, or abuse that may be causing you to self-mutilate.

This book will also answer questions you may have about self-mutilating behaviors. Most importantly, you'll find that you are not the only one who self-mutilates. Many others have suffered, but they have successfully stopped the behavior. You can, too.

What Are Self-Mutilating Behaviors?

You may find it hard to believe that anyone would purposely injure himself or herself. Or you might think that self-injury isn't a serious issue. However, self-mutilation is a growing problem. Experts believe that close to 2 million people in the United States may suffer from it. But because the research is new and the behavior is underreported, the numbers may be much higher.

Self-mutilation encompasses many behaviors, even some that don't leave visible scars on the body. Some of the most common forms of self-mutilating behaviors include cutting, hitting, burning, bone breaking, reinfecting wounds, and biting and digging. This book will take a close look at some of the different forms of self-mutilating behaviors to better understand their causes and consequences.

Types of Behaviors

Cutting

Research has shown that cutting is the most common form of self-mutilation. For many, the sight of blood is not only exciting, but comforting as well. Watching the blood flow is like watching all the pain go away.

A young girl called Andi cuts her arm when she's upset. She slides a knife over her arm until it bleeds. The sight of blood makes her feel better. It takes her mind off her emotional problems.

Andi doesn't cut herself because she wants to die. She does it to distract herself. She's scared to tell people because she thinks they will get angry or think she's crazy. At school, teachers react with concern and send her to the nurse. The nurse calls her parents as well as the hospital emergency room. Andi feels both annoyed and embarrassed. No one around Andi recognizes her behavior as self-mutilation. As a result, Andi isn't getting the treatment she needs.

People who cut themselves usually choose places on the body that aren't going to be obvious to others: usually arms and legs that can be covered up afterward. Some teens cut and scratch only their upper arms because even short sleeves will cover this part of their bodies. Some slash their chests because most garments will cover this area. Those who slash their wrists, which are less easily covered, may do so to communicate their pain to others or simply because they are acting on impulse.

Hitting

Java

Java was a student I had several years ago. When he was frustrated, he banged his head against the wall. He always tried to sit next to the wall. If all those seats were taken, Java banged his head on his desk.

The first time I became aware of this behavior, I was giving my students a test. Java apparently was stuck on one of the questions. He leaned his head back against the wall and quietly began to bang his head. He appeared to be in a trance.

A student sitting beside him looked over and whispered, "Hey you're going to hurt yourself."

Java's eyes seemed to refocus, and he stopped banging his head. Meanwhile, I walked over to his desk and asked if he needed some help.

Java wouldn't look me in the eyes. "I don't get this one," he said, pointing to a question.

I looked at the question and tried rephrasing it. After a couple of minutes, Java seemed to understand and began writing again. I walked back to my desk.

Another time our class was engaged in a heated role-play. Java was playing the part of a shopkeeper, while another student haggled with him over the price of an item. At one point, Java ran out of options for dealing with the problem. Frustrated, Java banged his head on his desk.

The other students seemed alarmed. "It's just a role-play," one of them said.

Java didn't seem to hear them. He kept banging his head until finally I raised my voice and told him to stop. His eyes refocused, and he sat up. "I'm so stupid," he said. "I can't think what to do next."

"Okay, class," I said, addressing the others. "Can any of you suggest ways to help Java deal with this negotiation?"

The students started offering suggestions, and Java appeared to be listening. I was worried, though, about his self-destructive behavior. He always seemed to take his frustration and confusion out on himself.

Java's was an unusual case. Most people who engage in headbanging and self-hitting don't do it where others can see them. Often, they're the ones

7

who come to school with reddened faces or recent bruising all over their arms. As a rule, they'll do their hitting and slapping in private and then wear long sleeves and other garments to hide the bruises. Some people become so used to this coping mechanism that they forget where they are, as Java did, and fall back into their pattern even in public.

Anthony

Anthony worked as a janitor on weekends to save money for college. He had trouble letting go of unpleasant thoughts. Whenever he started thinking about all the people at his workplace who left their trash for him to pick up, he'd get angry. The more he thought about it, the angrier he got. Finally, to get some relief from his overwhelming anger, he'd slap his own face. Initially, the sting from one or two slaps would startle the bad thoughts right out of him. However, as he resorted more and more to that coping mechanism when no one was around, he found he needed to hit himself again and again. His mother brought him to our agency for therapy the day his face was so red and battered that she had called the police. She thought he'd been beaten up and couldn't believe that he had done that much damage to himself.

Burning

Burning oneself, whether with cigarettes, cigarette lighters, or heated instruments, is a form of self-mutilating behavior. Some people take scalding hot showers or use handheld hair dryers to burn their skin.

Bone Breaking

Some teens engage in self-mutilation by actually smashing their arms against a wall or hard object in order to shatter their bones. They don't feel relief until they've cracked the bone. Other teens will use heavy objects to hit their legs or feet so they can break the bones.

Reinfecting Wounds

Some people keep reinfecting their wounds. Once a sore starts to heal, they open it again, exposing it to germs.

Biting and Digging

Digging into the skin, picking old scabs until they bleed, and biting oneself are all forms of self-mutilating behavior. Some people also dig at callouses until they bleed.

What Is Not Self-Mutilating Behavior?

Tattooing and Branding

Although tattooing and branding actually damage body tissue, they are not considered self-mutilating behaviors. Tattooing and branding are usually done to a person by someone else with the express purpose of adorning one's body. Secondly, someone doesn't usually get a tattoo or a brand to combat feelings too intense to deal with otherwise. Self-mutilators can't delay their need to self-mutilate, and tattooing and branding are generally not behaviors that can be undertaken at a moment's notice.

Body Piercing

Piercing different body parts may seem more like self-mutilation than tattooing does. However, while some

9

body piercing may seem excessive or inappropriate, people don't engage in it for the same reasons that self-mutilators hurt themselves. Getting pierced is most often done in an attempt to beautify the body.

Tension-Reducers

Anxiety is hard to handle, so some people distract themselves by doing seemingly self-destructive things like biting their fingernails or pulling their hair out. Biting nails isn't considered self-mutilation unless it is so severe that you actually need medical help. Hair-pulling can sometimes be a form of self-mutilation, but more often than not, it is just a compulsive, nervous habit.

Is It a Suicide Attempt?

Self-mutilators hurt themselves, not as an end in itself, but in order to relieve themselves of intense feelings or to create feelings when they feel numb inside. Because people engaging in self-inflicted injuries aren't trying to kill themselves, self-mutilators are not considered to be attempting suicide. Today, many doctors are able to distinguish between the two behaviors, which is important in ensuring proper treatment.

However, self-mutilation can result in accidental death. For example, some people who self-mutilate only mean to cut their wrists, to watch them bleed and feel as if their intense anger or sadness is pouring out of the wound along with the blood. This can be perceived by others as a suicide attempt. Some may even cut an artery and then can't stop the bleeding, resulting in death. The self-mutilator did not intend to kill him/herself.

He or she meant to rid himself or herself of unpleasant feelings, or to trade some physical pain for emotional pain. He or she is looking for a means of emotional survival.

The Cycle of Self-Inflicted Violence

Self-inflicted violence is not a one-time event. It often becomes a way of coping with life. Unpleasant feelings, such as anger and fear of abandonment, lead to a state of emotional tension. This tension requires the use of coping techniques. Some people develop the unhealthy coping technique of self-mutilation, which relieves the built-up tension. Relief becomes a positive reinforcer for the self-mutilation. If you self-mutilate, you may feel better for the moment, although shame and self-reproach may soon follow the immediate sensation of relief. The shame leads to more emotional tension and the cycle repeats itself.

Why Does Self-Mutilation Happen?

Research has shown that self-mutilating behaviors typically begin in adolescence, reach their peak in a person's twenties, and decrease with age. By the time someone is in his or her thirties, he or she is probably mature enough to have developed a better ability to tolerate uncomfortable feelings. Since the relief obtained from self-mutilating behaviors decreases with repetition, there is less reinforcement over time for this method of coping.

While there are similar patterns of self-mutilating behavior, several different reasons explain why a person self-mutilates. Some self-mutilate out of a fear of rejection, abandonment, or disappointment. This fear becomes overwhelming to the point where a person feels he or she has no control over the anxiety. The anxiety and fear increase until the person feels numb or empty, which is known as emotional depersonalization. In other words, the person is emotionally removed from his or her feelings. Self-mutilating is used as a way to resist and fight off this depersonalization.

In the book *Women Who Hurt Themselves,* author Dusty Miller outlines other motivations for self-mutilating behavior.

- To ease tension and anxiety

- To escape feelings of depression and emptiness

⮑ To escape feelings of numbness; many who self-mutilate say they do it to feel something, to reinforce that they are still alive.

⮑ As a continuation of previous abusive patterns

⮑ To relieve anger and aggression

⮑ To relieve intense emotional pain

⮑ To regain control over one's body

What is it that happens to some teenagers to make them need a self-destructive escape valve for handling strong feelings? Can a person who intentionally hurts him or herself be reacting to emotional stress? And what kind of issues contribute to emotional stress anyway?

Trauma Reenactment

People who've experienced serious trauma in their lives often engage in self-mutilating methods that recall earlier childhood abuse. This behavior is called trauma reenactment because the self-mutilator has incorporated the role of both abuser and victim into the behavior. While other forms of self-injury serve to distract the person, trauma reenactment continually reminds the person of the earlier abuse.

Since society tends to discourage girls from acting assertively, and girls who've survived trauma sometimes are very angry, they turn that rage inward and hurt themselves. Feelings of anger at the abuser prompt the violence; feelings of shame and a sense of being responsible for the abuse explain why they harm themselves. Dusty

13

Miller believes this may be the reason that self-mutilation is more common among females than males. Society encourages men to express their anger outwardly, so they are less likely to hurt themselves.

Emotional Stressors

One of the most important things about adolescence is that most teens want to fit in. They don't want to be "different" because people who are different stand out and get teased and hassled by their peers. The pressure to be like everyone else can be very intense and difficult to handle.

Zeb

Zeb was a transfer student to Central High School. His classmates thought he was a brain. He always seemed out of step with his peers. He didn't wear the right clothes, and he hung around with all the unpopular kids in ninth grade.

Zeb didn't care that he was out of sync with his peers until he had a crush on Mitzy, who sat in front of him in Algebra I. But Mitzy traveled in a different circle. She hung out with all the popular kids, and Zeb didn't know how to compete for her attention. He watched other kids who were in the so-called "cool" crowd. Most of them smoked and bragged about the drinking they did on weekends.

One day, Zeb got an older teenager to buy him some cigarettes and beer after school. He discovered that it was much easier to drink a beer than it was to smoke a cigarette. He actually enjoyed the taste of beer, and he liked the way he felt after he'd had a few beers. His grades started to drop when he didn't turn his homework in on time, but he wasn't as concerned about his grades as he was with Mitzy's opinion of him.

He tried talking to her in class but always got tongue-tied and couldn't finish a sentence. He was desperate to ask her out, and beer was the only thing that seemed to lessen his fear of embarrassing himself. So, he drank more and more. Finally, one afternoon after having a few beers, he worked up the courage to ask her out. He dialed her number carefully once he was sure his whole family had left the house.

"Mitzy," he said when she answered the phone on the third ring.

"Yes," she said.

"I wanted to invite you to the Valentine's dance Friday," he mumbled.

"Who are you?" she asked.

"Oh, this is Zeb Hardaman," he said.

"Zeb?" she asked as if she didn't recognize his name.

"I sit behind you in Algebra," he said.

"In Mr. Dill's class?" she asked.

"Yes, so do you think you can go to the Valentine's dance?" he said. He waited for her to reply.

"Oh, I'm already going," she said.

He was silent. What were you supposed to say anyway after someone you liked shot you down? Zeb took another long drink of his beer. "See you around then," he said.

He lit a cigarette and didn't care if it smelled up the house. He inhaled, and he coughed. Disgusted, he stared at the burning cigarette. Slowly, he turned the cigarette toward the skin on his left wrist. He brought the cigarette close. He touched his skin with the cigarette. Instantly, he drew back with the cigarette, but he smiled oddly when he saw his burned skin. It had not hurt that much, he thought. And besides, it didn't hurt half as much as hearing Mitzy turning him down. He flicked an ash on his arm and tried to see how long he could keep from brushing off the ash.

Peer Pressure

Not all teens feel this desperate about fitting in with their peers. However, it's very difficult to ignore peer pressure and not be influenced by it. Many people, including teens, feel a strong need to be like everyone else. It's hard to decide whether you want to do what everyone else is doing or obey your own values. Low self-esteem makes it even harder to stand on your own.

Sometimes, teens feel pressured to be thinner, smarter, or wealthier than they really are. Trying (and failing) to live up to other people's expectations can make you feel anger, anxiety, disappointment, and worse, self-disgust. Dealing with these feelings by developing healthy coping skills can help somone handle the problems of negative peer pressure.

Academic Pressures

Sometimes, it's not your peers who pressure you to live up to their expectations. Rather, it's your parents and teachers who urge you to meet their tough standards. Holding high expectations for you isn't always a bad thing, unless it's not something you want for yourself or it's not a goal you're capable of reaching.

Myra came from a family of overachievers. Succeeding academically was not just appreciated, it was expected. Myra spent many hours each night studying, but unfortunately, her efforts were not resulting in top grades.

She brought home her grades for the first semester of tenth grade. Three Bs, two Cs, and an A. She didn't want to show her grades to her father. She was worried he would be disappointed in her. Myra was angry because she knew she had worked hard throughout the semester.

"I really worked hard," Myra said, handing her father her report card.

"Bs and Cs?" he cried. "Since when are Bs and Cs any good?

"I got an A in art," she said, looking at her feet.

"So, who's going to care about art?" he said. "What's your problem? Aren't you studying enough?"

"I study every night," Myra said. "I just don't do well on tests."

"Then, let's get you a tutor," he said. "I'll call your school tomorrow; they must have plenty of kids who can help you, especially if I pay for it."

Myra sighed. "If that's what you want."

"I want all As," her father said. "If it costs me a fortune, then it's money well spent. You have no idea how important an education is. Bs and Cs won't get you into the college of your choice."

"Maybe I'm just not as smart as you think," Myra volunteered.

"Of course, you are," he said. "All your brothers and sisters are smart."

Myra felt torn. She wanted to live up to her father's expectations, but, at the same time, she felt Bs and Cs were good enough for her. Besides, she was more interested in art. Why couldn't her father accept that? Why did it matter so much to him anyway?

She knew she would get the tutor, and that she would have to study even harder to try to please her father. This depressed her. She knew she would work hard and still never measure up.

Romantic Breakups

Sometimes, teenagers have a hard time recovering from a breakup. They may attach themselves so strongly to their girlfriends or boyfriends that they feel they wouldn't have lives without them. Low self-esteem and inadequate coping skills can result in a number of strong, negative feelings such as anger, rejection, and grief.

Teens who've grown up without much stability in their lives may seek that stability in relationships. Once attached, they're not prepared when the objects of their affections fall out of love with them. Sometimes, the emotional pain of rejection feels worse than any physical pain you might experience.

Identity Issues

Teenagers often experiment with their identities, trying on different roles, casting off what doesn't feel right to them. Are they bright students, are they athletes, are they social butterflies? Sometimes, you try out different roles to find the one that fits.

The same applies to sexual identity. Sometimes, people know exactly who they are and who they find attractive. Sometimes, they aren't so sure about themselves or what types of people they like. Others know exactly who they are, but keep it a secret because family or friends would not approve of their lifestyles. If you don't feel good about yourself, what will you do with all those negative feelings? If you question your sexual orientation, you may condemn yourself or try to be something you aren't. Either way, the emotional pain can be overwhelming.

Losses

Life is full of losses. Divorce and death are the two main experiences of separation in a teenager's life. You may not be prepared to cope with the difficult feelings that erupt when faced with these kinds of losses. Young people often take these major events personally, feeling they are responsible for their parent's divorce. Or they believe the accident in which their parents died was somehow their fault—even if they were miles away at the time.

The early years, including the teen years, are a time of attachment and separation. Some attach better than others; some endure separation better. It depends on how capable you are of handling life's crises, and what type of crises have come your way. The less trauma you experience, the less you fear attachment and separation.

Loneliness and Isolation

Friends are a very important support system. It's natural to feel some emotional pain if you feel you don't have friends or people who care about you. Being lonely makes it hard to handle all the stress that can come along. If you are feeling lonely, you may be struggling with feelings of depression as well.

Sensitivity to Failure

Adolescence is a time of insecurity and pressure to succeed. It's not surprising that teenagers may be sensitive about failure. Failure means the possibility of losing approval, which can lead to feelings of isolation and depression.

Gordon

Gordon's father couldn't wait until football season started. He'd been the star running back in his day, and his picture still hung in the high school's front hall. Gordon had to walk by it every morning. He wasn't looking forward to football season.

All Gordon's father talked about in the weeks leading up to football tryouts was his plan to help out the team once Gordon joined it. It never occurred to him that Gordon couldn't make the team.

Gordon attended every tryout, but his heart wasn't in it. He was clumsy and skinny; he knew he didn't stand a chance. And if he didn't make the team, he didn't want to be the one to tell his father.

The day the team roster was posted, Gordon's name wasn't on it.

Gordon's stomach dropped. Would his father still help out if he wasn't on the team?

Gordon waited until after football practice before going home. If Gordon showed up too early, his father would automatically know he hadn't made the team. He wondered how long he could pretend he was on the team. His stomach turned over and over, and his head ached. When he got home, he spotted his father's car in the driveway.

He opened the screen door and took a deep breath. Suddenly he felt angry. Why was it such a big deal to get on the football team anyway?

"Your failure is home," Gordon shouted, as he slammed the door. He felt furious, but he was too scared to express that to his father. It was safer to take that anger out on himself.

Sexuality

Emotionally, teenagers aren't prepared for a sexual relationship, even if their hormones tell them they're physically ready. Being intimate is risky, especially these days when you can easily acquire a sexually transmitted disease, and an unplanned pregnancy can complicate your life and jeopardize hopes and dreams.

Alcohol and Drug Use

Some teens live very unstable lives. These teenagers may turn to drugs and alcohol to help them cope with emotional stress. However, when under the influence, they do things they wouldn't normally do. They may dare each other to cut or burn themselves. If they were sober or straight, they'd never engage in this behavior. But people lose their judgment when they drink and use drugs.

Emotionally unstable teenagers may have no one to show them how to handle troubling feelings; they are unusually sensitive to failure and easily pressured into doing things against their better judgment. These teenagers are the likeliest to self-mutilate because they don't have healthy ways of handling emotional pain.

Why People May Not Handle Feelings Well

Adolescents may not recognize or be prepared to talk about their feelings. Kids learn by observing what goes on in their families and then behave accordingly. If their parents never talk about their feelings in the family, kids aren't going to have healthy role models to copy. If parents don't know how to share their feelings, they can't teach this to their children.

Parents also may never have validated a child's feelings when he or she first tried to talk about them. Perhaps the parents ignored how the child felt, leaving the child feeling invisible, unnoticed. Perhaps the parents ridiculed or criticized the child for talking about his or her feelings. The child may have learned at an early age to suppress his or her feelings. However, without an appropriate outlet for expressing difficult emotions, children develop unhealthy coping behaviors.

Purpose of Self-Mutilating Behavior

You've just read about the emotional stressors that can precipitate uncomfortable feelings. Now, let's look at why people would actually want to hurt themselves because of these very powerful feelings. People tend to repeat the things that bring them relief from their pain. And for most self-mutilators, physical pain is far easier to deal with than emotional pain.

Physical Pain Versus Emotional Pain

Not seeing a better way to handle their feelings, self-mutilators finally choose the one thing that can overwhelm the emotional pain: physical pain. It's easier for self-mutilators to deal with physical wounds than to deal with the unseen pain they feel.

Libby

> Libby was working at a dry cleaner's shop when fire trucks and ambulances screeched by and turned onto her street.
>
> Then the phone rang. The manager answered and handed the phone to Libby. "It's for you," she said.
>
> Libby grabbed the phone. "Hello?"
>
> The color drained out of Libby's face. "What happened?" she asked. "No, wait, I'll be there."
>
> Libby threw the phone down. "I've got to get home," she said. "Mom's had an accident."
>
> "Of course," her manager said. "Is your mother okay?"
>
> Libby was feeling hysterical. "She's had an accident. She's had an accident," she repeated.
>
> "Libby, you shouldn't drive now; you're so upset."
>
> "I have to get home. My mom's hurt." Libby grabbed her purse and car keys and ran for the parking lot.
>
> Days after her mom's funeral, Libby sat in her room staring at the wall. Her mother hadn't really had an accident. She had put a gun to her head and fired, and if a neighbor hadn't gone to investigate, Libby would have been the one to find her when she came home that night.
>
> Blood was everywhere. Libby's Aunt Davelyn tried to wash it out of the carpet, but the stains were still

there. Libby rocked back and forth; she couldn't walk into the den anymore. It smelled of death.

They told Libby she wasn't completely alone. Aunt Davelyn would move in with her for a few weeks until they could straighten out matters (which probably meant selling the house and most of her mother's things). Libby thought about the money problems that had driven her mother to suicide. Was everything supposed to be better now? Was Libby's life supposed to roll along as before?

She had cried so much in the past few days, she couldn't cry anymore. She felt numb. This must be what it feels like to be in shock, she thought.

She drew a line down her arm with her fingernail file. It didn't hurt at all. How long had her mother wanted to die? She pressed harder with the nail file, and it pierced the skin. Although blood started to trickle down her skin, Libby still didn't feel anything. Libby dug into her arm harder. Angered, she stabbed at her arm, over and over until the sharp pain made her stop.

Her arm throbbed; blood ran down onto the carpet. Libby gazed blankly at her arm, not seeming to comprehend that she had done this to herself. The wounds hurt, but they brought her back to reality. "I've got to clean this up," she said. Washing and cleaning and bandaging the wound kept her from thinking about her mom's death. The hurt was worth it if she didn't have to feel emptiness and rage for at least a few minutes of each day.

Feelings

Self-mutilation is a way to express feelings such as shame, rage, and fear. It's also a way to cover up feelings by substituting physical pain for emotional pain. The teenager wants both to discharge unbearable feelings and to bury them. Self-mutilation is a dangerous way to accomplish both.

Cutting, burning, or disfiguring yourself are ways to express shame. What events could cause someone to feel so ashamed? Physical, emotional, and sexual abuse evoke feelings of shame because the victim often feels responsible for bringing on the abuse. Doing something disgusting to his or her body is the victim's way of shaming him- or herself and acting out the rage he or she feels toward the perpetrator of the abuse.

Some teens think that self-mutilation is a way to gain control over their feelings. Self-mutilators make themselves feel what they want to feel. Other people may have the power to make them feel hurt or ashamed, but they have the power to inflict pain. They simply inflict it on themselves.

A person who self-mutilates may think it's not acceptable to rant and rave when angry. Instead, she chooses to quietly express her anger by cutting herself. The cutting is her way of ranting and raving or expressing her anger. She does it in secret because expressing anger is not allowed in her household. She may feel she has gained a sense of control.

Hurting oneself can also be a way to get revenge. When Lawrence's girlfriend broke up with him, he slashed his wrist. Taking all that rage out on himself made him feel as if he were actually hurting his girlfriend. He was trying to destroy something she had once loved— him. At the same time, the cutting and bleeding took his mind off the terrible feeling of abandonment.

Creating Distance from Others

Sometimes, people engage in self-mutilating behavior because they want to scare off other people. Although they want to connect with others, many people are afraid of intimacy. If you get close to someone, you risk suffering if he or she leaves. For many, connection means the possibility of rejection. So, they cut on themselves because others are turned off by such behavior and stay away from them. While it hurts to be lonely, it also can feel safer. Self-mutilators who make their cutting public knowledge are usually trying to push people away. They do the very thing that will repel others; by hurting themselves, they get rid of pent up feelings and keep people at a distance at the same time.

A Way to Communicate

Sometimes, teenagers hurt themselves in ways that others can see because they want others to stop them. It's a cry for help.

Jeremy

Jeremy's father had deserted the family when Jeremy was born. Jeremy's mother didn't have much time for her son, and by the time he was a teenager, he was drinking and using drugs. His mother threatened to put him in counseling but never followed through. Then his mother bought him his own television set so he could watch his favorite shows whenever he wanted.

Jeremy was the envy of his friends. "Your mom will let you do anything," they'd say.

Jeremy would smile and admit he was pretty lucky,

26

but secretly he wondered if his mother even cared about him. Otherwise why would she let him get away with the stuff he did? She even knew about the times he skipped school; she'd told a neighbor, "Well, all boys go through this stage." And that was the end of it.

Jeremy kept pushing his mother by doing more things that were off limits. But she never seemed to care or set limits. The day he slashed his wrist and went over to show his friend what he'd done, he finally got someone's attention.

"Man, what did you do that for?" his friend said when he saw him.

"I don't know; I guess I was drunk."

"I've got to call an ambulance," his friend said.

"Go ahead," Jeremy said. "Maybe they'll have to call my mother out of a meeting."

A Way to Feel Alive

Some people hurt themselves because they've lost their ability to feel anything, and physical pain is better than numbness.

Clara

Clara was a client I saw years ago who was severely depressed. Because Clara experienced side effects when taking medication, the doctor took her off all prescriptions for a couple of weeks. In the meantime, Clara's depression increased. She called me one day and asked for an emergency appointment. When she came in, she looked calm and collected, not depressed and haggard like I'd expected.

Clara sat down quietly in one of my big chairs. She wasn't smiling, but she wasn't sad either.

"I was going to cut on myself," she said simply.

"Why?" I asked. It was the first thing that popped into my mind.

"Because I can't stand feeling this way," she said.

"What way?"

"Numb," she replied. "I don't feel anything anymore."

"And not feeling anything is worse than feeling depressed?" I asked.

"It's beyond depression," she said. "It's nothingness."

"But how does cutting yourself fix that?" I asked.

"It makes me feel something," she said.

"Pain," I said, following her thinking.

"It's better than this nothingness," she said.

"So, why did you call me?" I asked.

"I made you a promise, remember? If I wanted to hurt myself, I'd tell you. Well, I feel like I want to do it."

She looked so calm and serious. "Do you have anything to cut yourself with?" I asked.

"This," she said, and she handed me a scalpel.

"We need to hospitalize you," I said, "until you're feeling safe. Let's call your parents."

Nurturing the Self

For some people, it's not the cutting or burning that matters most. It's the nurturing that comes afterward. Creating a wound externalizes the emotional pain. It's something you can see. It's also something you can nurture and make better. For some teenagers, it's the only nurturing they can depend on.

Getting Attention and Fighting Boredom

Not all self-mutilators consciously realize they are coping with uncomfortable feelings by hurting themselves. Sometimes, they're only trying to rebel and to assert themselves. Carving on themselves is not socially acceptable, so publically engaging in this behavior is a way not to conform to society's expectations. Although hurting yourself isn't a healthy way to handle your negative feelings, disfiguring yourself and displaying it does make a statement: "See what I can do to myself" or "I can handle pain."

Sometimes, teenagers cut themselves for attention. Perhaps they are frustrated that someone else in the family is getting more of Mom and Dad's attention. Perhaps they believe no one cares about them unless they have proof in the form of affection or concern from others after they have self-mutilated. The teenager knows that cutting her arm should get a reaction (attention) and is willing to pay the price (pain) in order to get that reaction.

Some teens carve words in their arms because they're bored. The behavior is an unhealthy way to attempt to handle uncomfortable feelings.

Relief

There's another important reason some people cut themselves. Sometimes, self-mutilation causes a release of endorphins, the body's natural pain relievers. When someone is severely injured, endorphins are released to help prevent him or her from suffering. Scientists think that endorphins are released when people self-mutilate as well.

You feel good when endorphins are released, and

triggering pleasurable feelings is a strong reinforcement to continue a behavior. You might have started out expressing your anger by carving on your arm, only to discover that your self-mutilation triggered a natural high. Connecting the good feelings to your self-destructive behavior, you may do it again and again. Even though negative consequences—shame and injury—follow self-mutilating behaviors, the positive feelings are more closely connected to the experience. Whichever consequences are quickest to follow the act will be those that are the more reinforcing.

Other people practice self-mutilation because they claim it's the only way they can experience pleasure. These people often have higher threshholds for excitement and pain than most people, and so they must do more damage to feel more excitement. These self-mutilators are some of the hardest to treat because they don't see any reason to stop what they're doing.

Copying Others

Self-mutilating behaviors can also be observed and imitated. Young people who are sent to detention centers or hospitalized in psychiatric wards will be exposed to others who already practice self-mutilation. In these settings, there is no opportunity to self-mutilate in secret; thus, young people see others cutting or burning themselves openly. If the behaviors gain some secondary benefits, such as more attention from the staff or removal to a better environment, others might consider it rewarding. Some people begin to self-mutilate after having been around others who did it first.

Abuse and Emotional Trauma

When people have been severely abused, they can develop several serious disorders: borderline personality disorder, post-traumatic stress disorder, and multiple personality disorder (now called dissociative identity disorder). They may also self-mutilate as a way to deal with the trauma of the abuse. What most self-mutilators and people with personality disorders have in common is the ability to dissociate their minds from their bodies so that they don't seem to experience pain.

Trauma Reenactment

People who suffer from traumatic reenactment syndrome engage in self-mutilating behavior that represents the abuse they suffered in childhood. When children are repeatedly abused, and nothing is done to help them, they can take on the role of abuser, victim, and the nonprotecting bystander. Self-mutilation lets them act out the feelings of the abuser (by attacking themselves), the feelings of the victim (shame for what happened), and the feelings of the bystander (being powerless to stop this behavior).

Yvette

As a young girl, Yvette was repeatedly molested by her father. She dreaded the moment when her mother left each evening for work because she knew there was no one to keep her safe from her father. She never told anyone what her father was doing. She never screamed because her father would have struck her. Instead she would just drift away in her mind.

Yvette equated physical softness with vulnerability. She tried to erase any signs of her own femininity because she thought that female softness made women vulnerable to male battery. She played pool because she viewed it as a man's game, and she liked to slam the balls into the pockets. Whenever she lost a game, she berated herself. If she lost badly, the only thing that made her feel better was to go home and close herself in her room. There, she'd take out her knife and repeatedly stab her hand. She found herself floating away at these times, all the while hacking away at her hand. Eventually she would feel calm and would bandage her bloody hand and wipe the knife clean.

Yvette not only hurts herself; she reenacts her trauma over and over again. She stabs her hand. Stabbing herself allows her to reenact the trauma and experience the feelings of the key players: the rage of her father, the abuser; and her shame and violation as the victim. When she's upset and angry, she can't control the overwhelming need to stab herself, thus she incorporates the helplessness of her mother (the nonprotecting bystander) who leaves her alone with her father each night and is therefore powerless to stop the assaults.

Secrecy

Self-mutilation almost always takes place in secret. The self-mutilating teenager hurts herself in secret because she believes she is keeping a part of herself private, something that she couldn't do with her abuser.

Keeping her self-mutilation hidden becomes the same as keeping the sexual or physical abuse a secret. She still feels she's living up to her part of the bargain.

Shame and secrecy go together. The abuse victim frequently feels responsible for the abuse. It is too frightening to believe the adult loved her so little—abused her with no reason. She decides that she must have done something to make the abusing adult do this to her. Blaming herself is one way to regain some control over the situation. If she did something to provoke this mistreatment, then next time, she won't do that, she reasons. Since she feels responsible, and she thinks she must have been bad, she feels she deserves to be punished and hurt.

Relationships

Sometimes, because of repeated abuse, people get a distorted picture of relationships. The father who only spends time with his son when he beats him may cause the child to equate violence with connection. The mother who constantly belittles her daughter sets her up to expect ridicule in all relationships. Worse, a teen may use the self-mutilating behavior as a relationship of sorts. When he's alone and feeling unloved, he burns himself or cuts himself. That revives memories of his earlier abuse, and though the memories are painful, they feel positive because they remind him of his connection to the abuser. Hence, survivors of abuse and emotional trauma hurt themselves because it conjures up memories of connection. The self-mutilating behavior becomes a secret friend.

Juan

When Juan is feeling lonely, he likes to go to a secluded place in the woods behind his house. He brings his boom box and takes a steak knife from the kitchen drawer. He makes sure no one sees him leave, because they would try to stop him. Juan doesn't want to stop cutting himself. It's the only time he feels connected to the world.

Juan finds his favorite spot in the woods. The hemlocks stand so tightly together around him that they practically hide him from sight. He turns his boom box on softly and takes out the knife. His heart beats faster at the sight of the knife. He lifts his shirt up, revealing ugly scars in various stages of healing. He drags the knife across his skin.

Years ago, Juan's stepfather beat and cut him. He threw Juan around and spat on him. But every so often, when he was totally drunk, Juan's stepfather would scoop Juan out of his bed and cuddle with him on the couch. Those were the only times Juan felt loved or needed. After the cuddling, Juan's stepfather pulled out his knife and held it to Juan's chest. He left faint red lines across Juan's chest and threatened to cut him all the way through if Juan ever told anyone about the abuse. Juan never told, partly because he was ashamed, but also because he felt he had a special, secret relationship with this otherwise brutal man.

After the divorce, Juan continued to cut his chest because it made him feel loved. The cutting took the place of his stepfather's cuddling. They became one and the same. A part of Juan knew the behavior was *unhealthy; that's why he kept it secret. If anyone found out, they'd make him stop, and then he'd have nothing for comfort.*

Post-Traumatic Stress Disorder (PTSD)

People who've been chronically abused (whether sexually or physically) can develop post-traumatic stress disorder (PTSD). Whenever they feel anxious, they may dissociate (the way they did during the original trauma) and hurt themselves. It's a way of coping with the feelings of fear and anger. One client who witnessed a horrific accident when she was young methodically pushes her fingers into her eyes when stressed, as if she's literally trying to blind herself.

Dissociation

The ability to dissociate, or stop being aware of the present, makes it easier for a person to self-mutilate. When you dissociate, you go somewhere else in your head and aren't aware of what you're doing to yourself. Therefore, you don't feel any pain. The danger with dissociating lies in being unaware of how seriously you may be hurting yourself. If you don't feel any pain, and aren't aware of how much you might be bleeding or burning, you could cause much more damage than you intended.

Companion Problems of Self-Inflicted Violence

Self-mutilators often experience problems with eating disorders and substance abuse. Consequently, treatment for self-mutilation can include treatment for companion problems. It's important to be aware of behaviors that accompany self-mutilation in order to understand what you or others who engage in this harmful behavior are experiencing and how to seek help. Some of these behaviors are outlined here.

Anorexia

Anorexia is an eating disorder in which a person starves herself. She perceives herself as overweight no matter how thin she may be. Like self-mutilation, a person who starves herself keeps it a secret. The behavior is often well-established by the time it comes to others' attention. And usually, the damage is quite severe.

Not only will a person suffering from anorexia become weak from not eating, she will have dull hair and possibly damaged teeth. Her system can be out of balance because she's no longer taking in adequate amounts of vitamins and minerals. If done long enough, anorexia can lead to heart damage from electrolyte imbalance.

Because self-starvation is very harmful, anorexia is sometimes considered a form of self-mutilating behavior. Sometimes, people with anorexia engage in other forms of self-injury, specifically cutting or burning themselves.

The dynamics may be similar for the person who cuts herself and the person who starves herself. Both may be wanting to gain some control over a life they see as "out of control." By inflicting injury on themselves, they feel as if they're reasserting control over their lives. In their way of thinking, at least, *they* are responsible for the pain and hurt.

The professional who treats an anoretic must make a proper diagnosis. Is the person starving herself in order to gain control over her life, or is the person punishing herself and her feelings through starvation? One behavior has to do with an eating disorder; the other has more to do with self-mutilation.

Bulimia

Bulimia is another eating disorder. A bulimic tries to maintain a low body weight by purging food from the body to compensate for eating binges. Bulimia is very destructive to the body.

Sharon

Sharon was initially diagnosed with anorexia and was hospitalized. She looked average in size—not too skinny. She tried eating as little as possible. It was a constant struggle between us. She tried to lose weight, while I, as her therapist, tried to get her to gain weight or at least maintain her weight. After a while, Sharon decided the only way to get off the ward was to go along with my wishes. She started to eat regular meals.

I thought that meant she was getting better. She was eating a decent amount of food now, but she continued to lose weight according to the scales. How could she still be losing weight when I sat with her during every meal?

Later I learned that she threw up after every meal. So, I didn't allow her the opportunity to vomit after eating. However, she still lost weight even though she ate. How? She called her relatives and friends and told them she was constipated. She talked all of them into bringing her laxatives, and she took all that they brought her. She had used laxatives to purge herself of calories before, and had developed a tolerance for them, so she needed massive amounts to purge herself now.

In therapy sessions, Sharon told me how her father had sexually abused her when she was much younger. "It just makes me sick to think about it," she once told me. After several readmissions to the hospital, I understood why she binged and purged. The bingeing was her way to soothe and feed herself; the purging was her way to get rid of her ugly experiences. She knew she was physically harming her body. When you throw up repeatedly, or bring on diarrhea, precious minerals are washed out of your body at the same time. This can lead to electrolyte imbalance and heart damage. It can also result in a reflex action where you end up vomiting after every meal you eat, even if you don't want to.

Sharon felt dirty and ashamed of the sexual abuse. Bingeing and purging in secret allowed her to continue

*experiencing the shame and humiliation that she part-
ly believed she deserved. Many people with eating disorders are purposely hurting themselves, not simply
trying to maintain a decent weight. It's more about self-
inflicted violence than it is about eating or not eating,
so the victim needs as much attention paid to the self-
mutilating behavior as to the eating disorder itself.*

Compulsive Eating

Compulsive eating is similar to bulimia in that it involves
bingeing behavior. However, compulsive eaters do not
purge. Intentionally eating too much food or the wrong
kinds of food to gain weight is a way to hurt yourself. Obesity confirms low self esteem; furthermore, it can cause diabetes and complicate other health problems. Obesity can
also lead directly to heart problems.

But compulsive eating isn't always a sign of self-inflicted
violence. People eat for different reasons. Sometimes, the
dynamics have more to do with wanting to punish yourself
(self-mutilation) than to soothe yourself. The latter is strictly
an eating disorder, as long as it's the food itself that's sooth-
ing you. If you feel soothed because you physically hurt
afterward, that constitutes self-inflicted violence.

Substance Abuse

Those of you who have tried to get drunk on purpose
because you were mad about something are resorting to
self-mutilating behavior. You're intentionally hurting yourself either because you think you deserve the punishment or
because you're trying to alter your mood through chemicals.

Sometimes the substance abuse problem is inadvertent. The angry teenager doesn't quite have the courage to act out his anger, so he gets drunk or gets high first. Under the influence, he's more likely to do "crazy" things and less likely to feel any pain at the time. In this case, the desire to self-mutilate prompted (or combined with) the substance abuse problem.

Anorexia, bulimia, compulsive eating, and substance abuse can all be considered companion manifestations of self-mutilating behavior when they're done to hurt the body to experience relief. This is also true when the behavior's goal is to manage uncomfortable feelings.

Why do we even have to categorize the behavior? The treatment is different for someone who drinks, eats, starves, or purges in order to self-mutilate. People who are actually self-mutilators will never fully recover, no matter what the program, if their self-mutilating behavior isn't addressed. What usually happens is that they'll trade one form of self-mutilating behavior for another. The bulimic may overcome his or her bingeing and purging but turn to cutting him- or herself to create physical pain.

The Effects of
Self-Mutilating Behavior

People who hurt themselves say shame, anger, and self-disgust propel them to do it. Once they've hurt themselves, they feel even more shame and self-disgust. Self-mutilating teenagers suffer from low self-esteem, and they do not have effective coping skills to deal with the unpleasant feelings confronting them. Instead of problem-solving, they turn their confusion and anger onto themselves. The self-injurious behavior confirms their low opinion of themselves and exposes them to more shame. They may regret what they've done and promise not to repeat the behavior. They often hide what they've done from others to spare themselves others' negative reactions. Even years later, when many teenagers have outgrown their self-mutilating behavior, they may be embarrassed for others to see what they once did to their bodies.

Physical Consequences

Cutting and Burning

The most obvious consequence of cutting yourself is bleeding to death. Teenagers don't engage in this behavior because they want to die; many are dealing with anger, loneliness, and other uncomfortable feelings. They cut themselves to feel physical pain that will overshadow their emotional pain. However, there's always the risk of cutting an artery and inadvertently bleeding to death.

Another serious consequence is scarring. Cutting yourself until you bleed leaves a scar behind. The more cuts you make, the more scars will cover your arms and legs. Even superficial cuts will leave scars. Cuts made repeatedly in the same place will leave bigger and uglier scars. Scars do not fade away entirely. They are constant reminders of self-injurious behavior.

> One day during a soccer game, the weather was so warm that people were pushing up their sleeves or taking off their sweatshirts. When Rita took off her jacket, several girls close by gasped. Her arms were crisscrossed with old scars. Her daughter, Courtney, was embarrassed. "Put your jacket back on," she yelled to her mom.
>
> Rita yelled back, "I'm hot."
>
> Courtney's face reddened. "The other parents are looking at you," she whispered.
>
> Rita couldn't hear her.
>
> Another teammate looked over at Courtney. "Was your mother in an accident or something? How'd she get all those scars?"
>
> Courtney missed the ball as it went whizzing past. "She was in an accident a long time ago."
>
> At the water break, Courtney told her mother to put her jacket back on. "The kids can see your scars. Doesn't that embarrass you?"
>
> Courtney's mother shrugged. "This happened in another lifetime," she said. "Maybe kids will see my scars and realize how uncool they look twenty years later."

Cuts can also get infected. When that happens, medical attention is required because antibiotics (the medicine necessary to cure an infection) aren't always available over the counter. If you're a diabetic and a cutter, you run an even greater risk of infection that could lead to losing the limb.

Burns leave scars, too. First, they scab over while they're healing, then when the scab drops off, a scar remains. Burns can also get infected, so they're the type of self-mutilation that can draw attention to yourself.

Poisoning

Some people who self-mutilate do so by drinking poison or overdosing. Some overdoses are worse than others. Many chemicals burn the esophagus and stomach. Once burned, there's nothing that can be done to reverse the damage. And since most chemicals are processed through the liver, an overdose damages the liver as well as other body parts.

Some people instantly regret their decision to overdose or poison themselves with chemicals. Unfortunately, once they've injested the materials, there's often nothing doctors can do to repair the damage. You can't always be given charcoal to absorb the poison. Likewise, you can't always have your stomach pumped or be made to vomit, because irritant chemicals will do twice as much damage coming back up your esophagus.

Damage from Eating Disorders

Eating disorders are sometimes considered forms of self-mutilation. Anorexia causes damage through starvation. Bulimia wreaks havoc on the body from bingeing and purging.

Purging means either forced vomiting or excessive use of laxatives to induce diarrhea. When you vomit or have diarrhea, you risk dehydration because it entails a major loss of body fluids. You don't just lose calories. When you're dehydrated, your skin dries out, and you become constipated. Minerals get washed out with the body fluids causing a life-threatening imbalance for some people. Dehydration also leads to bone deterioration as well as teeth and hair damage.

Forced vomiting can damage your esophagus (as regurgitated stomach contents are very acidic) and destroy the enamel on your teeth. When you make yourself throw up after every meal, your body gets accustomed to the action and will begin to automatically regurgitate any meal without any extra help from the bulimic.

Using laxatives to purge your body of unwanted calories does not cause reflexive reactions. Instead of having bowel movements more readily, you will have increasing difficulty. Eventually, you will not be able to have a bowel movement without first taking an enormous amount of laxatives. The loss of bodily fluids will reinforce the constipation problem.

Bingeing and Sugar Abuse

If you binge but don't purge, you are physically stressing your body. When you eat food, your body changes the food into glucose. The pancreas produces insulin to help turn the glucose in the bloodstream into fuel that cells can use. Once the insulin has processed the glucose, you'll feel hungry again. The more sugar eaten, the more insulin is produced to counteract the sugar. Sugar is processed quickly, which leads to hunger faster than do other foods.

When a bulimic person binges on sugar, her pancreas produces a large amount of insulin to process the sugar. If she then vomits what she's eaten, she gets rid of most of the sugar, but the insulin remains circulating in her bloodstream. This may trigger a crash, symptoms of which include weakness, dizziness, irritability, and rapid mood changes.

This abuse of sugar may contribute to two dangerous conditions: hypoglycemia and diabetes. Hypoglycemia results when blood levels of glucose drop too low to fuel the body's activity. You may experience anxiety or rapid mood changes in addition to feeling dizzy, cold, and clammy. Diabetes is a potentially life-threatening disorder in which a person either no longer produces insulin or isn't able to use it to process sugar out of the bloodstream. The diabetic has to take medication (either pills or insulin shots) to replace the insulin the pancreas can no longer produce. At this time, there is no cure for diabetes, but many treatment options exist.

Clearly, overeating as well as bingeing and purging have severe physical consequences for the person intent on taking out anger on him- or herself.

Substance Abuse

Drug and alcohol abuse are considered companion manifestations of self-mutilation. Many people engage in this behavior when they don't know how to handle their feelings. Unfortunately, there are physical consequences to substance abuse. Addiction and overdose are serious results. It is not easy to break an addiction. What may have started out as a way to handle emotional pain turns into a behavior that's difficult to give up and physically damaging to the body.

The problem with some drugs is that they depress (slow down) bodily functions. If taken in sufficient quantity, they can ultimately depress breathing. Other drugs act as stimulants, while still others can cause you to hallucinate or become violently psychotic. Some drug users have unintentionally killed themselves when all they were looking for was an escape from emotional pain.

Alcohol and other drugs will also damage your liver and stomach. Alcohol is processed through the liver; when your liver can no longer process the amount of alcohol it receives, it deteriorates. In addition, substance abusers (particularly drinkers) get stomach trouble such as ulcers, and gastric problems. Too much alcohol is actually a poison, and poisons affect all parts of your body because they travel through your bloodstream.

Brain cells can be destroyed by alcohol and other drugs and are not rejuvenated. You are born with all the brain cells you will ever need. Once you destroy them, they are not replaced. Brain damage causes confusion, forgetfulness, poor judgment, and personality changes.

Biochemical Changes

People who thrive on dangerous activities can actually create biochemical changes in their bodies. Eventually their threshhold for excitement and arousal increases, and they have to keep engaging in dangerous behavior to feel "normal." People who self-mutilate, particularly those who cut themselves, may eventually train their bodies to depend on the release of endorphins whenever they cut.

Even though it's not a positive activity, it becomes stimulating and is repeated. In effect, a person becomes addicted to this kind of unnatural "high."

Accidental Death
Ultimately, the danger with self-mutilating behavior is that the person can take it too far. Superficial cuts can heal, but a person can quickly bleed to death with severed arteries. Getting addicted to self-injurious behavior can lead to serious injury and even death. Overdoses, accidental poisonings, electrolyte imbalances, and heart attacks can lead to unintentional death. What might have started in anger, boredom, frustration, or depression can end in death.

Effect of Self-Mutilation on Others

Self-mutilating behavior exists on a continuum. Its effect on others depends on the severity of the behavior as well as how often it occurs. Someone who doesn't conceal a multitude of scars in various stages of healing will provoke a much different reaction from the person who has slashed her wrist for the first time.

We present ourselves to others three different ways: by what we say (our verbal communication), how we act (our nonverbal communication), and how we look (our symbolic communication). People draw their first impressions from our symbolic communication, and multiple scars that appear self-inflicted make a definite statement. This isn't to say that symbolic communication is accurate communication; however, it's what people see first and on what they base their perceptions. Being shocked by it, they may make unfair judgments about the person.

Other People's Reactions to Self-Mutilation
Some people recoil in disgust. Others are shocked and just want to stay away from the self-mutilator because they don't know how to help. Some are angry and believe the victim is being manipulative, while others are scared to be around these people, feeling as if the self-injurious behavior will be catching.

Donald

Donald was a seventeen-year-old high school student who cut his wrist whenever he felt out of control. He never cut so deeply that he caused serious damage, but he sometimes had to go to the emergency room for stitches and bandages. His parents grew exhausted reacting to his repeated self-mutilation; they took him to counselors, and they talked to all his teachers. Nothing seemed to make a difference; Donald still cut on himself, and they all felt powerless to stop him.

Donald's sister resented all the attention he commanded in the household. If his parents weren't taking him to the emergency room, they were talking to each other about how to monitor him more closely. Donald's behavior controlled all the people in his household. His parents felt powerless, and his sister felt ignored. His sister was embarrassed because her friends knew what Donald did, yet she sometimes worried that he might kill himself accidentally. She felt guilty, but sometimes she also felt relieved at that thought.

Sometimes, self-mutilators hurt themselves because they want to provoke a reaction of disgust and annoyance. They want to keep people at a distance, and cutting on themselves serves as a way to push people away. If they are public with their behavior, they know the reactions will be negative, especially if it is a pattern. People don't seem to have much tolerance for destructive behavior they don't understand.

Generally, most people don't like to make themselves vulnerable. Getting close to a person who behaves in a self-harming fashion makes one vulnerable. If they care about this self-harming person, they risk getting attached and feeling powerless to help him, possibly losing him in the end. Many people try to avoid taking these types of emotional risks.

Family members and friends may react with concern at the first sign of self-mutilating behavior. If the behavior continues despite their efforts to help out, they grow weary of the effort. They withdraw. Many people assume a person is either mentally disturbed or suicidal if she cuts on herself. It's difficult to deal with a self-mutilator, and most people find themselves unprepared to handle or understand this destructive behavior.

Janet

Janet had been dating Everett for a year. Lately, she started to resent all the things he did that at first seemed endearing. He had carved her name into his arm, and she thought that was romantic. After a while, though, she decided it was embarrassing because her friends wondered what other weird things he did. His intensity about life, and especially their relationship, frightened her. She decided they both needed to date other people, which was really her way of saying she wanted out of the relationship. His response to her announcement scared her. "If you find someone else, I'll kill myself," he threatened.

Janet didn't know what to do. Everett had always been so intense; that's what attracted her to him in the first place. But now that characteristic was no longer appealing; it was suffocating her. She wondered if he would really kill himself.

Scared, Janet desperately wanted to get out of the relationship. But at the same time, she was afraid to do anything that might cause him more emotional distress. She even started to worry that he might hurt her as well as himself. The more cuts she saw on his arms, the more frightened she became, convinced he was either suicidal or homicidal or both. She wished there was someone to talk to about this but didn't know how or where to ask for help.

Some people may feel more angry than frightened when dealing with a self-mutilator. They feel they're being manipulated, and they don't like feeling out of control. They resent the self-mutilator for making them feel guilty for wanting to get out of the relationship.

Charlaine

Charlaine did her cutting in secret, usually in the bathroom at school. She wore long sleeves so no one would find out. She knew no one would understand.

One afternoon while Charlaine was sitting with her friend Alison in the library, her sleeve unexpectedly slid up to expose her wrist and several fresh scratches. Alison recoiled when she saw them. "Ouch," she said. "What did you do?"

Charlaine yanked her sleeve down over her scratches. "I got cut and just picked the scabs," she said.

Alison reached over to grab her arm. "How'd you get those cuts?" she asked.

Charlaine wiggled her arm free. "It's nothing," she said. "I think I cut it on some bramble bushes."

Alison frowned. "I'm not stupid," she said. "Did you do that on purpose?"

Charlaine feigned shock. "Are you crazy?" she asked. "I just pick my scabs."

"Then let me see your wrist," Alison said.

Charlaine started to pack up her books. "I've got to get going," she said.

"You didn't want me to know," Alison said.

"Only because I'm embarrassed," Charlaine said. "It's kind of babyish to pick your scabs until they bleed."

"It looked more like you'd cut yourself with a knife."

Charlaine's face reddened. "That's crazy," she said.

"I know," Alison said.

"I didn't cut myself," Charlaine protested.

"Let me look at it and see," Alison said.

Charlaine looked at her friend. She wondered if she could explain the cutting to Alison. She wanted to tell her, but she was afraid Alison would make her get help. She didn't want to stop cutting. She didn't think she was crazy, but she just knew she couldn't explain all of this to Alison. "Just lay off it," Charlaine said, getting up and leaving the library.

Alison persisted with Charlaine, and eventually Charlaine admitted she sometimes cut on herself. "It's no big deal," she said.

Alison was worried. "You could really do some damage," she said.

"Well, I don't," Charlaine said.

"Look, I'm really concerned about you," Alison said.

"Then, leave me alone about it," Charlaine said.

"Why do you do it?" Alison asked.

"It's just something I feel like doing at the time."

"Yes, but why?"

"You wouldn't understand," Charlaine said.

"I'll try," Alison said.

"Okay, well, cutting my wrist calms me down." She looked up at Alison. "You don't get it, do you?"

Alison looked confused. "I don't think it's normal."

"Oh, so I'm crazy, huh?"

"I didn't say crazy. Obviously cutting on your own arm isn't healthy. Besides, you can't feel that great about it because you hide it."

"It's because people like you don't understand," Charlaine said.

Alison was frustrated and worried. Charlaine was doing something that certainly seemed abnormal. But she didn't want Alison's help. She didn't want to change.

Alison felt helpless and eventually became angry. Her anger led to avoidance, and her relationship with Charlaine ended.

The Rescuer Mentality

Some people are drawn to self-mutilators because they see such people as needing to be rescued. Some self-mutilators get into unhealthy relationships with rescuers; they don't want to stop their behavior (or perhaps they feel they can't stop it), but at the same time, they feel relieved whenever a rescuer responds to them. Eventually, one or the other tires of the relationship. The victim may tire of all the attention, and may no longer need someone watching over him or her. Likewise, the rescuer may tire of rescuing a person who never seems to stop needing help.

A person with the rescuer mentality likes to take care of others, and she likes being in control. This makes her feel needed and important. The problem arises when the victim rejects the help, or the rescuer expects progress, and the victim doesn't make any. That's when one or the other will tire of the dynamics of the relationship.

The Family's Role

Sometimes, families can perpetuate a member's self-mutilating behavior by maintaining the secret (out of shame or confusion), by discounting the seriousness of the behavior, or by threatening and lecturing the individual. Threats will only cause more secrecy; they rarely remedy the self-injurious behavior. Families quite often feel helpless when faced with a member's self-mutilation. Since the behavior doesn't make sense to them, they try different ways to get it to stop. Of course, without an understanding of the purpose of this behavior, families can't make it stop.

Self-mutilation is a way some teenagers choose to

handle their overwhelming negative feelings. Forcing them to give it up won't work but will drive them into engaging in it with greater secrecy.

Some families essentially condone the behavior by not discussing it. They may prefer not to know what's going on, believing that what they don't know won't hurt them. By not reacting to their children's behavior, they send the message that they don't care.

Finally, parents and siblings may be reluctant to consider the self-mutilator's problem as a "family problem." Seeing it solely as the self-mutilator's problem keeps it an individual problem; families don't then see how their own behavior contributes to the problem, sustains it, or exacerbates the problem. Chances are, self-mutilators who are unable to express their feelings in a healthy way haven't had role models to show them how.

How Professionals React

Professionals who deal with self-mutilating teenagers may use lecturing as a way to convince the teen to change his or her behavior. Unfortunately, as parents discover, lecturing is not very effective. The self-mutilator assumes the adult doesn't understand what they're going through and refuses to listen.

Lydia

Lydia burned herself with cigarettes. When teachers realized what she was doing to herself, they sent her to the guidance office. The guidance counselors sent her to therapy because they felt the problem was bigger than they could handle in the school setting. When the *behavior persisted, some teachers threatened her with detention and an alternative school.*

Lydia showed up for softball practice one afternoon, and her coach suggested they have a little talk.

"Not another lecture," Lydia groaned.

"Have you been getting a lot of lectures?" her coach asked.

"Everyone has a message for me," Lydia said. "I already know that no one thinks I'm normal."

"Well, as your coach, I'm concerned about your behavior."

"Don't lecture me," Lydia whined. "I can't take another lecture."

"Okay, I won't talk to you like a parent, and I won't talk to you like a student who needs detention. I'll speak to you as a coach. I'm concerned about the team. I need to have serious athletes. People with emotional problems don't make good athletes."

"What are you saying? Are you kicking me off the team?" Lydia asked.

"I'm suggesting you get some help for your self-mutilating behavior. You'll be better for it, and the team will be better for it."

"That's still a lecture," Lydia said.

Professionals, like teachers and coaches, will probably offer lectures because they're concerned about your behavior. They may not understand the behavior; they may be scared of it to some extent, and they expect you to try to get better. Initially, they might sympathize with you, but sympathy gives way to impatience if you refuse to seek help to control your behavior.

An experienced therapist knows that self-mutilators can't stop hurting themselves overnight. After all, it's the self-mutilating behavior that calms the anxiety. Stopping the mutilation leaves the patient without any way of keeping calm. A good therapist understands the importance of the symptoms and knows that the patient needs to learn new coping mechanisms, and that takes time. Only in the context of a trusting relationship can the self-mutilator explore his need to hurt himself and learn to stop the behavior.

Engaging in self-mutilating behavior will make some people afraid of you; it will turn some people off because the physical signs are disturbing to see. It will frustrate people who feel helpless and unable to keep you safe. That frustration will cause some to get angry and others to avoid you. Some people will want to rescue you; others will want to control you and get you to "act right." Rarely, though, will people be nonchalant about self-mutilating behavior when they're aware of it. Intentionally hurting yourself is bound to cause shock and concern. It's a serious condition, and one that can be addressed and successfully treated.

Treatment Options

If you can't seem to control your self-mutilating behavior on your own, or you're actually suicidal, you need to seek professional help. Some people consider therapy or hospitalization as a form of "giving up." But good therapists are like good coaches—they don't tell you how to live; good therapists guide you and support you along the way.

Teenagers who've suffered emotional trauma (which includes getting caught in a natural disaster, like a tornado, fire, or flood, or enduring chronic sexual or physical abuse) need to learn how to manage their overwhelming feelings of fright, loss, and rage. Most of the time, these feelings are simply too overpowering for people to handle on their own.

Likewise, if you don't know how to stop self-mutilating, although you're disgusted with your behavior, you may need to talk with a therapist. It's not a matter of someone telling you to stop and then you are able to comply. Therapists understand that your self-mutilating behavior serves a purpose for you. To simply admonish you to give it up would only force you to do something else equally destructive. Let's first consider who the therapists are and how you'd go about finding one.

Types of Therapists

While there are many different kinds of therapists available, the professional community tries to ensure their competence through the practice of licensure or board certification. Therapists who are board certified (doctors) or licensed have passed national exams and practiced under supervision for a certain number of years. Should you question their ethics, you can turn to their licensing boards for help. Licensing boards can censure their actions if warranted and revoke their licenses. There are many unlicensed therapists, though, who practice at community mental health centers under the supervision of licensed therapists. That's because unlicensed practitioners have to fulfill a two-year supervision requirement for licensure.

A psychiatrist is a medical doctor who has completed a residency in psychiatry. A psychiatrist is the only therapist allowed to prescribe medication that may be needed to manage some forms of mental illness or self-destructive behavior. A psychiatrist is the most expensive therapist to see, so more and more insurance companies are suggesting psychiatrists restrict their practices to prescribing medication and limiting the time spent in psychotherapy.

A psychologist is someone with either a Ph.D. in psychology or an Ed.D., which is a degree in educational and counseling psychology. Other psychologists have master's degrees. Psychologists have additional training in administering and interpreting tests, which can be a valuable part of treatment. The Ph.D. psychologists are expensive, although their rates may fluctuate from $100 an hour to $150 an hour. Most insurance companies compensate for the bulk of psychological services, as long as you're not seen more often than the insurance company believes is necessary.

Clinical social workers make up the bulk of therapists. They will either possess a Ph.D. or more likely an MSW (master's in social work). Many are also licensed clinical social workers, which means they all passed a rigorous national exam and completed two years of supervised practice. Many insurance companies prefer social workers because they possess the expertise yet don't charge as much as psychologists and psychiatrists. Their rates usually start at $80 an hour, depending on where they practice. Community mental health centers always have sliding scale fees (based on one's ability to pay).

Other professional counselors have at least a master's degree in a mental health field, often counseling or human relations. Some may gain licensure as Licensed Professional Counselors (LPCs) or Licensed Marriage and Family Counselors (LMFCs). Many insurance companies will recognize and reimburse for these professionals. All insurance companies expect a therapist to have at least a master's degree in the mental health field.

Choosing a Therapist

In seeking help, you will want an experienced, competent professional who has worked with self-mutilating clients. On top of that, though, you want someone with whom you feel comfortable. If you're going to invest in a process and get intimately involved, you want someone you respect and like, regardless of gender or age. And it certainly isn't necessary for your therapist to be a recovering self-mutilator. Therapists are trained to understand your suffering.

However, don't make a quick judgment of your therapist. Give yourself a few sessions before you decide to drop out or switch therapists. Therapy is not meant to be a fun experience. Therapy is hard work because you're taking a look at unpleasant situations and uncomfortable feelings in order to learn to deal with them. You may be grateful for the therapy later, but at the time, it's challenging. Just because you resist coming to therapy doesn't mean you've got a bad therapist. Therapy is about changing, and most people are resistant to change.

What Do You Do in Therapy?

People in therapy mostly talk. You talk about your family dynamics; you talk about your relationships with people, and what you think about adults.

Will the therapist make you talk about your self-mutilating behavior? That's a hard question to answer with a simple yes or no. Yes, your therapist will eventually get around to discussing the ways you purposely hurt yourself, but not until you have established a trusting relationship, which can take months. You're not going to want to share the purpose of your self-mutilation if you don't trust the therapist to understand. He realizes that, so he won't pressure you to discuss or discard the behavior until you're ready. If the therapist doesn't learn what the behavior means to you, he will not know how to end the behavior safely.

Will he make you give up self-mutilating? The goal is to curb self-destructive behavior, but he won't demand that you give it up before you're ready. Self-mutilating behavior is a stress reducer; the therapist and client will work to find healthier ways to handle the stress first. The experienced therapist may talk to you about the feelings leading up to your self-mutilation; he may suggest ways to act out the impulse without actually hurting yourself as a first step to stopping. Some therapists suggest their clients draw on their arms with a bright red marker when they want to cut themselves. This is just a step toward stopping the behavior. Ultimately the goal is to redirect your anger and frustration to healthy outlets.

Hospitalization

Hospitalization (whether in a regular medical center, a private psychiatric hospital, or a state hospital) is a last resort measure. In a hospital, you'll have less freedom to move around and more supervision. The goal is to keep you safe, preventing the opportunity to hurt yourself.

When you are an inpatient, you will probably receive individual as well as group therapy. Sometimes, depending on the facility, your assigned therapist will conduct family therapy sessions to take a look at how your family reacts and supports your behavior. Being hospitalized doesn't necesarily mean you'll receive medication, but it's a possibility to help curb your self-destructive impulses.

Once you're able to function without 24-hour supervision, the hospital will refer you to an outpatient therapist for continued therapy. Insurance companies do not authorize lengthy hospital stays, so hospital administrators are sensitive to that. If you don't have insurance, you may have to go to the inpatient wing of your local mental health center or to a state hospital.

The SAFE Program

The SAFE (Self Abuse Finally Ends) alternative program is the only inpatient treatment center in the United States that specifically treats self-injurers. Established in 1985 at Rock Creek Center, a general psychiatric hospital in Lemont, Illinois, it has helped many self-mutilators learn how to change their behavior. Ninety-nine percent of its patients are women. Here the staff treat the self-abusing patient in an inpatient setting. in order to participate in the program, patients sign a NO HARM contract stating they will not hurt themselves while there. Treatment consists of multiple group therapy sessions and family therapy sessions to explore the feelings that precipitate the patient's urge to self-mutilate.

Other Therapy Techniques

Whether in a hospital or in outpatient therapy, you first learn how to delay your urges to self-mutilate, and then delay the behavior for increasingly longer periods of time until you're able to give it up.

Therapists will teach you to talk out your feelings (anger, sadness, or hurt) rather than act them out. And if the staff sees you continuing to self-mutilate, they will take steps to keep you safe rather than punish you. Seclusion rooms are not meant to be used as a form of punishment, and leather restraints are rarely used in any psychiatric setting anymore.

Social Stigma of Getting Treatment

Some people are afraid to go into a hospital because they think everyone else will assume they're crazy. Unfortunately, you can't control what other people think about you. Maybe they will think you're unstable, but their assessment shouldn't enter into your decision to get help for yourself.

Some people are afraid to go into a hospital because they assume all the other patients are crazy. Undoubtedly, you will see more seriously disturbed patients, but the staff is there to keep you all safe—mental illness is not contagious. You may be locked on a ward in some cases, but you retain your right to make phone calls and have visitors. You'll most likely be searched for sharp objects because of your self-mutilating history, but psychiatric aides and nurses are trained to be helpful not punitive. A hospital stay should not be a negative experience—if you're suicidal, it's the safest option.

When You Don't Want Treatment

What happens if you don't want to get treatment, but your parents are making you get it anyway? Therapists can be reluctant to work with clients who don't want their help. But they understand that sometimes clients really do want help; they just don't want to cooperate with their parents' wishes.

If the courts order you to go to therapy, you have to keep the appointments. The courts can't require you to talk or to change, but you may find that the therapist is an interested human being who can offer you time and consideration.

Drug and Alcohol Programs

Since some teenagers engage in self-mutilation when they're drunk or high, treatment has to address the substance abuse problem first. Many teenagers will be surprised to discover it's not that easy to quit drinking or using other drugs. Alcoholics Anonymous groups don't always appeal to the teenager who doesn't consider himself to be like other addicts. So, many times the abusing teenager goes through a substance abuse program (whether inpatient or outpatient) to tackle the problem of the drugs before addressing the self-mutilation. Adolescent drug treatment programs exist in every major city; you can consult your local phone book or nearest hospital for information on these programs.

Cost of Therapy

Treatment is expensive, but there are ways to cover the costs when you don't have a lot of money. All accredited programs will be reimbursable through your insurance company. Check with your parents' insurance coverage to find out which program or therapist it recommends. Sometimes, insurance companies will not cover aspects of treatment for the self-mutilator because they claim the injury was self-inflicted. If your insurance won't cover your treatment, or you don't have insurance, seek help through the nearest mental health center. These centers will charge you according to your ability to pay. Sometimes Medicaid will cover the costs if you are already receiving disability checks.

Medications Used in Treatment

In some cases, doctors recommend medication to help manage the symptoms associated with self-mutilation. There's no magic pill that will change the self-mutilator overnight, but there are different kinds of medication that will target specific symptoms that may be contributing to the self-mutilating behavior.

Depression

There are essentially three different kinds of medication used to treat severe depression. None of them is addictive medication. If you are diagnosed with severe depression, your doctor might prescribe MAO inhibitors, tricyclics, or selective serotonin reuptake inhibitors, called SSRIs. Because of the way they act and their potential side effects, it's important to understand the differences among these antidepressants.

Serotonin and norepinephrine are the two major brain chemicals that modulate mood. Antidepressant medications work on increasing the amounts of these particular chemicals, but they do it in different ways.

MAO is the name of an enzyme in the body that breaks down and reduces the amount of serotonin in the brain. Therefore, doctors prescribe antidepressants called MAO inhibitors because they prevent this enzyme from doing its job of breaking down the serotonin. With more serotonin in your system, your mood is improved. Parnate is a MAO inhibitor antidepressant.

The medicine, taken orally, will not cure self-mutilating behavior by itself; however, its job is to reduce depression.

You still need therapy to address the problem of your self-mutilation because that behavior served a purpose for you or has become a habit.

Antidepressants are not addictive, which means you do not build up a tolerance for the drug requiring more and more of it to achieve the same effect, or experience painful withdrawal when you stop taking it. They merely keep the chemicals in your brain in proper balance. Of course, there are side effects to all drugs; the problem with MAO inhibitors is that they do not mix well with other substances such as central nervous system depressants as well as certain dairy products. Because the combination can be lethal, doctors don't usually recommend this type of antidepressant to someone unlikely to follow a strict diet.

Tricyclics are the second type of antidepressant and are considered by many to be the "older generation" medications. That simply means they've been around the longest. These drugs target both norepinephrine and serotonin, and because they affect both chemicals, they have the side effect of stimulating appetite. Some people don't like these medications because they lead to weight gain. However, with tricyclics you don't have to worry so much about drug interactions, which makes them safer to use than MAO inhibitors. Examples of tricyclics are amitriptyline, imipramine, desipramine, and trazedone. You need to take these pills daily for at least three to four weeks before you see any relief from depression. Once they've built up to a therapeutic level in your bloodstream, they will begin to affect your brain chemicals. Unlike anti-anxiety medications, you cannot take these pills whenever you feel depressed. You must take them as prescribed, and eventually taper off under a doctor's supervision, rather than suddenly stop taking them.

The newest types of antidepressants are the selective serotonin reuptake inhibitors, called the SSRIs. They specifically target serotonin and increase the level of this brain chemical by keeping the neuron (brain cell) from drawing the serotonin back up into the cell. When serotonin stays around longer in the area between the neurons, it enhances mood and combats depression. Fewer side effects are associated with SSRIs; they don't lead to as much dry mouth and weight gain as other medications do. However, some SSRIs may upset your stomach; people with agitated depressions can become violent, although doctors monitor patients and would see the signs of that behavior before it got out of control. Another good thing is that these medications also have a calming effect on people, so irritability and anger, which often lead to self-mutilating behavior, are lessened. Examples of SSRIs are Prozac (fluoxetine), Luvox (fluvoxamine), Paxil (paroxetine), and Zoloft (sertraline).

No Magic Pill

Remember, though, that medication alone won't cure your behavior. You still need to learn why you dealt with unpleasant feelings by hurting yourself. Therapy and medicine together can be very effective. And bear in mind that you can't take someone else's medication and expect to get the same results. Just because you feel depressed doesn't mean you can take your friend's antidepressant when you haven't seen a doctor yourself. You always need to be supervised while on antidepressant medication.

Medication isn't the solution to the problem of self-mutilation unless it's strictly behavior in response to a mental disorder, such as obsessive compulsive disorder, bipolar disorder, and schizophrenia (discussed in Chapter 7). Medication is only part of the solution, and it only helps with certain symptoms. In short, there is no magic pill available, so treatment can involve hospitalization, psychotherapy, and learning assertiveness techniques and better anger management skills. As a rule, there's no single reason a person will self-injure. The more serious the intent, though, the more likely both therapy and medication will be needed.

Self-Help Measures

Despite engaging in self-mutilating behavior, not all teens need to seek counseling. The rebelliousness and need to shock often goes away as teens learn to handle stress and loss in more positive ways. The depression and low self-esteem that prompts some self-mutilating behavior can be relieved with better conflict resolution skills and assertiveness training.

Identifying Sources of Stress

The first step to dealing with stress is to pinpoint the source of the stress. Are you being pressured to succeed in subjects or sports that aren't your strengths? Are your parents fighting and making your home an uncomfortable place to live? Are your friends pressuring you to do things you don't think you should? Are you able to say no to your friends?

Once you've made the connection, you can do one of two things: you can confront the problem or you can avoid it. Unfortunately, avoiding, denying, or accommodating a problem lead to frustration. Frustration in turn can lead to venting the feeling on yourself in the form of self-mutilating behavior.

You can confront the conflict in two different ways: one

is to use good problem-solving skills, which usually leads to satisfaction and better self-esteem. The second way is to act aggressively, though this is just as destructive as avoiding the conflict in the first place. You intimidate others and make enemies. Making enemies and losing approval leads to low self-esteem and feelings of depression.

Clearly, there are times when conflict should be avoided. Choosing not to fight when you're outnumbered can be a smart move. However, it's the unresolved conflicts that fester and cause the uncomfortable feelings. Even if your negative feelings are stirred up when your parents fight frequently and you don't feel it's right to jump into the fight, you can still identify the source of your stress (your parents' fighting) and confront it. Confronting in this particular case may mean talking out your feelings with a third party or asking an adult who can intervene for you. It doesn't mean you have to confront these yourself.

People who've been abused (physically or emotionally) may be afraid to confront because they've learned that direct confrontation is unsafe. However, handling stress means confronting the problem, not running from it. Talking to a trusted adult, a guidance counselor, or a close relative can give you ideas of how you might address the problem. Doing nothing makes you feel powerless and angry. Sometimes, those feelings will propel you to hurt yourself rather than vent in a healthy way.

Tolerating Feelings

In order to solve a problem, you have to be able to tolerate the feelings that arise out of the problem. That doesn't mean you have to live with the feelings the rest of your life, and it doesn't mean you have to like the feelings. But in order to tolerate discomfort in life, you have to be able to tolerate some uncomfortable feelings at least until you can do something about the situation. Cutting yourself is not a healthy way of tolerating feelings.

Sometimes, you're going to feel anxious, angry, or sad. Those feelings are actually useful emotions because they alert us that something is wrong in our lives. Masking the feeling (by covering the emotional pain with physical pain) doesn't remedy the situation. It merely allows you to remain in the unpleasant situation instead of doing something about it.

Think about what feelings make you most uncomfortable. Is it sadness, anger, fear, or joy? Some people are more afraid of happy feelings than sad feelings because they expect the happiness to be short-lived and a forecast to bad events. Or they don't think they deserve to be happy. Once you've identitifed the feelings that make you most uncomfortable, try to make yourself tolerate that feeling a few more minutes each day. Start out with five minutes. Promise yourself you'll do something about it after five minutes, but during that time, just concentrate on the awful feeling. Sometimes, when you focus on something totally, it loses its power over you—it ceases to scare you. Try to be objective. Describe the feeling and how your stomach reacts, or if your fingers go cold. You won't die from an uncomfortable feeling, even though it might feel that way. See if you can identify what part of the feeling is so scary. Then try to tolerate uncomfortable feelings for longer and longer periods. Eventually you should be able to tolerate uncomfortable feelings for an hour or more. By that point, you'll see that it's possible to survive unpleasant feelings.

Handling Feelings[1]

It's important to learn how to handle the feelings effectively once you're able to tolerate them. Anger is commonly the most uncomfortable feeling for people to handle. That's probably because most people think anger is bad. Anger is neither bad nor good. It simply exists. If you're not afraid of it, you can use it effectively to change an unpleasant situation into a better one.

Once you recognize you're angry (and some people actually laugh when they're mad), make sure you know the source of your anger. If you're really angry that your mother wouldn't let you go to the dance on Friday night, don't pick a fight with your teacher simply because it's easier to fight with her than with your mother.

Some people get so angry, they can't see straight or deal with their anger productively. If this happens to you, teach yourself to tolerate the feeling of anger and then find positive ways to calm yourself. Self-mutilation isn't the answer. Instead, do something that will make you tired out, but won't hurt you or increase your anger. People who hit walls or break dishes are being destructive, and that causes anger to grow. Running or other forms of exercise are good ways to tire yourself out without hurting yourself. Running takes time, too, so often after a good long run, your perspective will return. Playing racquetball is a good way to tire yourself out, but other people like to "shoot hoops" to calm down, and others swim laps. Whatever positive activity drains your fury and gives you enough time to think more clearly will work.

Once you've dealt with your feeling of anger, the next step is to confront the person or situation that made you angry in the first place. You won't solve the problem by complaining to all your other friends and not confronting the person who angers you. That person is often the only one who can help you change the situation.

Figure out what's making you angry and think of a satisfactory solution. It's frustrating to both sides when you confront someone with your anger, and he or she asks you what can be done, and you shrug and say, "I don't know." It's more effective to have a solution in mind, whether it's an apology you want or a change in behavior.

Use assertive communication when expressing what's bothering you. Describe the behavior that upsets you and how it makes you feel (bearing in mind that anger usually masks hurt and embarrassment). For example, say, "When you make jokes about the way I look, it hurts my feelings and then I don't want to be around you." The other person will then either suggest a change, apologize, or ask you what you'd like to have happen. If she persists with the joking, simply continue using assertive communication. "When you keep making jokes, I'm angry because it feels like you're not taking me seriously."

You'll be surprised how good it can feel to tackle a problem head on, even though it seems easier just to run from it. By facing it, you don't have to turn all those bad feelings against yourself.

Handling Sadness and Loss

Many people prefer to feel angry rather than sad because sadness hurts so much. Fifteen years ago when my son died, I was numb with shock and then very, very angry. That anger kept me alive because I refused to give in to my grief. The anger kept me from facing my almost unbearable feeling of loss at a time when I just wasn't able to handle it. Gradually I grew stronger and was able to tolerate the horrible sadness, but for a long time I tried not to feel that emotional pain. It simply hurt too much.

A lot of people don't like to cry either. Crying makes them feel sadder, so they resist. What they don't realize is that crying may hurt a lot in the begining, but it releases the pain. When faced with loss, you feel sad, and when you're sad, it's natural to cry. Crying does hurt, but the only way to get rid of the pain is to let it go.

You may not always feel like crying. Still you can talk about how you're feeling to friends and trusted adults. Talking about your feelings keeps you from acting them out.

Handling Fear and Anxiety

For most people, not knowing what to do about a situation is part of what's so intolerable about feeling afraid and anxious. That's why it's so important to learn at an early age how to think up alternate plans. If you think there's only one way to solve a problem, you're back to square one feeling afraid and anxious again if that plan backfires. I urge all of my clients to come up with Plan A, and then Plan B (if A won't work), and Plan C (if B falls through). If you don't put all hope in one plan, you have energy left to try another option.

Thinking up alternate plans takes time and effort, but your time is better spent thinking up possible solutions than hurting yourself to mask the fear and anxiety. Besides, coming up with plans A, B, and C gets easier the more you practice. Even if you don't have to resort to Plan B or C, you can feel more sure of yourself knowing you have other available options.

Handling Negative Thoughts

Usually it's our feelings about an event that bother us the most, not the actual event. For example, let's say you're walking down the hall and pass one of your teachers. She frowns at you, or maybe she just doesn't smile at you. If you're a negative thinker, you'll probably jump to a negative conclusion. "She didn't smile at me because she graded our exams, and I failed."

One negative thought usually leads to another. Next thing you know, you're acting as if those negative thoughts are actually facts. "She probably doesn't think I should be in her class because I'm not smart enough." "I probably should get out of her class before she tells me to." "I'm just not good in math anyway, so maybe I should quit taking math classes."

The result is that the negative thinker acts on her feelings and not the actual event. She assumes the worst and she believes it's always her fault.

But isn't it possible that the teacher was thinking about something else and never even saw her student? Isn't it equally possible that she wasn't feeling well? By not considering these possibilities, the negative thinker saw only one explanation for the lack of a smile. Now, when the student goes to class, she's going to act as if that belief is a fact, which may lead the teacher to see the student in an unfavorable light.

To counter negative thoughts, try breaking your automatic tendency to jump to the worst possible conclusion. When something happens to upset you, write it down. A= the actual event. Then record all your thoughts about this event. B= your beliefs and feelings. Note them all. The more you put down, the more irrational it's likely they'll appear in print. C= the consequences. You will probably find that because of your beliefs about A, you're either angry or depressed.

However, don't stop yet. D= your chance to dispute those negative beliefs. Find plausible alternatives for the upsetting event; note any evidence contrary to your assumption. Negative people get into all or nothing thinking ("If she didn't smile at me, she must hate me"), or they assume everything is their fault. They catastrophize, thinking that one bad moment forecasts a lifetime of bad moments. They maximize any mistakes and minimize anything positive they did. Some have a negative spin on the world, and they go looking for the negative and overlook the positive. These are all distortions. If you are diligent about recording all your thoughts, you'll soon spot the distortions and can tell yourself, "Oh, I'm overgeneralizing again."

Disputing the belief is the most important part of this cognitive technique because if you don't believe the worst, you're able to anticipate better things.

Here's an example of the A-B-C-D approach.

A = My best friend didn't eat lunch with me today.

B = She's mad at me about something. She's found a
new friend. She doesn't want to eat lunch with
me anymore.

C = I avoid places where I'll run into her, and I don't
call her after school the way I usually do. I'm
depressed and angry because she used to be my
best friend.

D = Maybe she got tied up in class and couldn't make
it to lunch. Maybe she was sick and went home.
(Those are alternative explanations.) She wasn't
there eating with anyone else, so she doesn't necessarily have a new friend. I didn't even see her
this morning, so we had no occasion to fight.
(Those are evidence-to-the-contrary explanations.)

The goal is to try to stop dwelling on the negative. You
didn't get depressed only because your friend didn't eat
lunch with you (the actual event). Rather, you got
depressed because you believed the negative thoughts
you had explaining the event. The point is, if you're a negative thinker, make sure you investigate your assumptions
before accepting them as facts.

Obsessive Worrying

People who obsessively brood about things will sometimes resort to self-mutilation to stop the thoughts. The
physical pain interferes with the repetitive thoughts, and

the person gains temporary relief. Unfortunately, he has a more serious problem to contend with at that point: using self-mutilation to deal with obsessive thoughts.

Some people are natural-born worriers, and the worrying drives them crazy. If they are suffering from obsessive compulsive disorder (discussed in the next chapter), medication can help them control their obsessive thinking, but certain behavioral techniques can help, too.

I've created a form to give to my obsessive worriers. It looks like this:

⇒ What is the worst thing that can happen?

⇒ How likely is it to happen?

⇒ If more than 30 percent, devise plans A, B, C to deal with it.

My clients then record the things that cause them to stay awake worrying at night or cause them great anxiety during the day. Then, they rate how much they actually believe the event will happen. Most people will reasonably assess the likelihood of events when they are recorded on paper. If the percentage is higher than 30 percent, they need to prepare for the event to happen, which means devising different solutions. However, if the percentage is less than 50 percent, remember that there's less than a 50/50 chance it'll happen in the first place. No need obsessing over something if it's unlikely not to happen. However, you're still going to be prepared; often just knowing that you have several options available in case the negative event happens will lessen your worrying.

Healthy Highs

Self-mutilation can become an addiction to some people because of the flood of endorphins released. It isn't wise to risk injury and death for a high that you can get other ways. Your body will also release endorphins when you run for long distances or engage in other sports. Working out also develops your self-esteem, which is added insurance against hurting yourself.

If you aren't interested in sports, you can fill your time with other positive activities: hobbies, clubs, volunteer work, or a part-time job. Self-mutilators who cut on themselves because they are bored will have less time for the harmful activity if they're doing something productive with their time. Contributing to society will also increase your self-esteem. Look for opportunities to volunteer with schools, charities, or hospitals.

Letting People Help You

Therapists can help you when professional help is needed. However, lots of people who aren't professionals can be a support system for you too. These are stable people who will encourage you to talk out your feelings rather than act them out in hurtful ways. These are people who will help you think up positive ways to handle your problems.

Take a good look at your relationships. Are you involved with healthy people, or do your friends and family support each other in self-mutilating practices? It's harder to break out of this behavior if you're surrounded by peers who do the same thing. What's the focus of your relationship? Drugs? Drinking? Cutting on yourself? These types of friendships are unhealthy. It may be time to reevaluate your group of friends when you decide to get help.

Finally, find healthy role models if your own parents are not supporting you. Look to other adults in your community who can serve as mentors. Seek out and learn from teachers, ministers, coaches, or healthy adult relatives.

Having effective coping skills means being able to confront the sources of your stress, not running from them or hurting yourself to take your mind off them. Many self-mutilators can give up this behavior with only the help of a good support system and the ability to tolerate and handle their feelings.

---

[1] Ideas based on David Burns's book: *The Feeling Good Handbook.* (NY: William Morrow & Co., 1989.)

More Severe Disorders

Sometimes, self-mutilating behavior is a component of a more severe disorder. In that case, professional help (and possibly hospitalization) is needed. Medical research has divided self-mutilating behaviors into three broad types: typical self-inflicted violence (which includes scenarios we've already discussed that are considered a result of psychological and emotional problems), psychotic self-inflicted violence (which includes behavior that occurs because the person is out of touch with reality), and organic self-inflicted violence (which occurs because the person suffers from brain damage or mental retardation).

Obsessive Compulsive Disorder

A person who suffers from obsessive compulsive disorder (OCD) has to perform certain activities over and over to manage his anxiety. These repetitious activities are called compulsions. Some people experience obsessive thoughts in addition to their compulsions. They simply can't get certain thoughts out of their heads.

Janetta and Adam
   Janetta has obsessive compulsive disorder. When she is stressed, she pulls her eyelashes out. She

knows she is hurting herself, but she can't stop herself. She was starting to pull out hair on her head, and because she couldn't stop the behavior by willpower alone, she sought therapy.

Her brother Adam is also obsessive compulsive. He worked in a manufacturing plant on the assembly line. It was a routinized job which gave him plenty of time to lose himself in thought. Sometimes songs would go through his head, and the more he tried to get them out of his head, the more they taunted him. Eventually, he would become unable to keep up with the assembly line, he'd get frustrated, and slap himself. Slapping himself served as a temporary thought-stopping measure. But it didn't keep the repetitive thoughts away for long. So, he'd slap himself again harder and harder to knock the songs out of his head. Some days when Adam emerged from work, his face would be swollen from all the slapping. His supervisor wondered if he was getting into fights, so he started monitoring him. When he saw that Adam was actually the source of his own abuse, he sent him to the company's Employee Assistance Program counselor to get some help.

Treatment for OCD

Medication is often helpful in combatting obsessive compulsive disorder. Low levels of the brain chemical serotonin have been linked to people with OCD. Therefore, medication that affects the serotonin levels disrupts the repetitious behavior and obsessive thoughts that accompany OCD. People who pull their hair out benefit from high doses of SSRIs. Once the brain chemical balance is restored, the self-mutilating behavior stops. Anafranil is the medication of choice for people with OCD; however, it has some unpleasant side effects, including weight gain and headaches. People also respond well to Prozac and Luvox (although in doses higher than what's used to treat depression).

How long will you have to take this medication? Your doctor will help you decide this. He or she may suggest staying on the medication for six months and then tapering off to see if self-mutilating symptoms return. There are no dangers yet associated with long-term use of SSRIs, although serotonin syndrome (which can be fatal) can develop if taking too high a dose of SSRIs for too long a period.

Borderline Personality Disorder

A person diagnosed with borderline personality disorder (BPD) has a pattern of instability in his relationships and self-image and also may be impulsive. He may make efforts to avoid abandonment, real or imagined.

A person diagnosed with borderline personality disorder (BPD) frequently uses self-mutilation as a way to deal with feelings of emptiness, anger, and fears of abandonment. This person has developed a maladaptive way of relating to the world since early childhood. BPD can be caused by early childhood neglect, abuse, or trauma. The result is that the person thinks in terms of black and white, which particularly affects her relationships with others. She starts out idolizing someone and ends up detesting him. If you are in a relationship with someone with BPD, usually you feel overwhelmed by the neediness of the person with BPD.

When relationships deteriorate, the person with BPD may resort to self-mutilation to ease the emotional pain of rejection and abandonment.

Treatment for Borderline Personality Disorder

Depending on the severity of the disorder and the degree of self-mutilation, a combination of medication (to reduce depression, irritability, and impulsivity) and psychotherapy is needed. People who have seriously injured themselves, even though they didn't intend to kill themselves, may need hospitalization until their moods have stabilized. Psychotherapy aims at helping the person understand his intense relationships and helping him to become less needy and dependent on another person for his sense of well-being. Additionally, therapists help people with borderline personality disorder find positive alternatives to cope with their overwhelming feelings.

Bipolar Disorder

Bipolar disorder is the new name for manic depression. A person with this disorder may or may not experience psychotic symptoms as well. Most notably, the person swings between two extremes of moods: mania and depression. His moods are extreme, and they are nearly impossible to moderate on his own.

Most people with bipolar disorder require medication at some point, and they will probably need it for life to even out their moods. Some people with bipolar disorder self-mutilate when they're on a manic high; others are more likely to make suicidal gestures when they're on the depressed end of the continuum. The problem with giving an antidepressant to this person is that it can precipitate a manic episode. Some people can tolerate antidepressants as long as the medications are given in addition to a mood stabilizing drug, such as lithium, tegretol, or valproic acid. Valproic acid is also a good choice for people with anger problems, and self-mutilators are often people who take their anger out on themselves.

Dissociative Identity Disorder

People with dissociative identity disorder, formerly called multiple personality disorder, develop distinct personalities as if they were separate identities. Invariably, these people learned at an early age to dissociate when they were being abused. When a person dissociates, she simply goes away in her mind to some place else so that she is no longer aware of what is happening to her at that particular moment. People with dissociative identity disorder have taken dissociation to the extreme. When they dissociate, another personality steps in to take their place. They can become this other personality for minutes or hours or days, and the original personality has no idea of what has taken place while she was gone. The main personality, called the host, is sent away (or goes to sleep) when an alter personality steps in to handle a situation. The victim of dissociative identity disorder can have as few as two alters or as many as one hundred. It's quite conceivable that one of the alter personalities will intentionally harm another, not realizing that all the personalities share the same body. The person who cuts herself and is unaware that she is responsible may be telling the truth. She may have a dissociative disorder in which one identity is trying to destroy another.

Cordelia
Cordelia was diagnosed with dissociative identity disorder. She was not initially aware of her twenty odd personalities. One of her personality fragments was a little boy who knew about Cordelia's experience of abuse. The other personalities didn't want Cordelia (the host personality) to know their secret. They didn't want her seeking help because they feared being destroyed by the therapist. But once her diagnosis was made, Cordelia began to make progress.

Treatment for Dissociative Identity Disorder

Unfortunately, psychiatrists haven't found any particularly effective medications for the treatment of dissociative identity disorder. Often, SSRIs are used to manage the level of irritablity and anger. Valproic acid has also been used to some extent to control rage attacks, and sometimes major tranquilizers are used in very small doses to manage the dissociative aspects of the disorder. In the long run, though, the most effective treatment is intensive psychotherapy (talk therapy) to help the individual integrate or coordinate the personalities in her system.

Schizophrenia and Psychotic Behavior

Schizophrenia is the most serious psychotic disorder a person can have. The schizophrenic has a thought disturbance that often causes him or her to hear voices that aren't there or to believe certain false ideas. These ideas, usually paranoid and based on the irrational assumption that people are out to get you, are called delusions.

Schizophrenics who self-mutilate usually do so because voices inside their heads command them to hurt themselves. Sometimes they know that they are hurting themselves, but they feel powerless to resist the voices. Other times, they think they are cutting out some horrible part of themselves, not cutting into an artery. They might believe they're destroying the devil, instead of burning their flesh with cigarettes.

Gina

Gina couldn't handle her feelings and believed voices talked to her. When she was upset or hearing voices, she often cut herself with sharp objects, so we had to be especially watchful of her on the ward. Sometimes, she hurt herself because "the voices inside her head" told her to do it. She knew what she was doing, and she knew it could kill her. However, the voices were demanding and persistent. She could not resist them.

Gina often drank poison to harm herself. It's not easy to find bottles of poison on a hospital ward, so Gina swallowed any liquid she could find that would hurt her. Once, she drank bleach when a cleaning woman accidentally left her mop bucket and supplies outside the bathroom. Another time Gina drank perfume.

The schizophrenic self-mutilates for reasons far more serious than an inability to deal with uncomfortable feelings.

The schizophrenic actually believes he has to obey his inner commands, no matter how irrational they appear. Thus, the treatment for self-mutilation in someone suffering from schizophrenia or other psychotic disorders would be different from someone who is overwhelmed by uncomfortable feelings.

Schizophrenia and other forms of psychotic behavior are extreme and don't account for most self-mutilating behavior. Most self-mutilators don't hear voices or don't have multiple alters. They are simply dealing with unpleasant feelings the best way they know how, despite the consequences.

Treatment for Psychotic Thinking

When someone is psychotic (whether it's drug-induced or a result of a psychiatric disorder), it means she's out of touch with reality. Doctors theorize that people with this condition have too much of the brain chemical dopamine. Medications used to treat people who are psychotic work because they block the release and uptake of dopamine, thus decreasing the levels. The various major tranquilizers (or antipsychotics) used today include Risperdal, Clozaril, Zyprexa, Mellaril, Navane, and Haldol. The first three are relatively new medications with fewer of the side effects of the older tranquilizers, such as muscle stiffness, drooling, dry mouth, and the possiblity of tardive dyskinesia (an irreversible condition of involuntary movements). Clozaril, though, must be closely monitored with weekly blood checks to make sure the immune system is functioning as it should. The drug's worst side effect is that it can decrease white blood cell count which could leave the body vulnerable to infections.

How long will these medications be taken? The person suffering with schizophrenia will probably have to take medication the rest of her life, as there is no cure at the moment. Fortunately, there are other medications (Artane, Cogentin, and Benadryl) that are specifically prescribed to combat the side effects of the major tranquilizers so that people will be more likely to comply with long-term use.

However, someone who becomes psychotic from experimenting with drugs may only need to take the major tranquilizers temporarily until the psychosis wears off. Some people who experience psychotic symptoms when depressed may only need to take major tranquilizers for a few months until the depression subsides. Because these medications are so powerful, they are not prescribed haphazardly. Nor are they addictive. Doctors (particularly psychiatrists) know when and how to prescribe these drugs. If someone self-mutilates because he is psychotic, a doctor will prescribe major tranquilizers before any psychotherapy can be effective. In some cases, the person needs to be hospitalized first until an effective dose of the medication can be found.

Creating Illness: Munchausen's Syndrome

Munchausen's syndrome is not a common disorder, but it is appropriately considered a form of self-mutilation. Munchausen's syndrome is a psychological disorder that causes a person to hurt herself (it's more likely to be a female phenomenon) on purpose in order to get medical treatment. People hurt themselves by creating symptoms of a physical illness. Unlike hypochondriacs, Munchausen sufferers actually have the physical symptoms of an illness. They do require medical treatment; it's just that they bring the symptoms on themselves.

Symptoms and Behavior

People who have Munchausen's syndrome deliberately create their symptoms in order to receive medical treatment. They might contaminate their blood with dirty needles to mimic a disease; they might put animal blood in their urine to make it appear they had bloody urine. They might heat thermometers to register a fever; they might put sugar in their urine to feign diabetes. Some people purposely punch themselves in the abdomen simulating an attack of appendicitis. Some intentionally cause themselves repeated infections. If a doctor seems to suspect that they could be causing their illness, Munchausen syndrome sufferers come up with different symptoms that confound the doctor even more.

Doctors are forever trying to diagnose and explain the symptoms of the Munchausen sufferer. For some doctors, it's easier to hunt for the mystery illness than to believe the victim brought these symptoms on herself. People are malingering when they pretend to be sick so that they can get out of school or win financial compensation. But Munchausen sufferers are not malingering. They have no purpose other than to be a patient and get treatment. They go from hospital to hospital seeking painful forms of treatment.

An Explanation of Causes

Munchausen's syndrome is not an easy disorder to study. Some theorize that Munchausen sufferers are so exquisitely sensitive to emotional pain that they go to great lengths to hurt their bodies in an effort to change the focus of the pain. They believe the sufferer is reacting to real or imagined loss.

Some theorize that a victim of Munchausen's syndrome undoubtedly suffered childhood abuse and probably over-identified with an abused parent. The surgeries and invasive diagnostic tests are ways to abuse themselves and get comfort at the same time. Most Munchausen sufferers were also hospitalized at an early age and remembered the hospital and their relationships with their doctors as positive experiences.

Munchausen's syndrome is not common, but it does exist. If you recognize the symptoms in yourself or a loved one, it's vital to seek psychiatric help. Research has found that early detection is essential to the patient. The Munchausen sufferer doesn't necessarily want to die, but that may happen if he succeeds in hurting his body one too many times. In addition, some Munchausen sufferers will inflict injury on their children, continuing the pattern with them. That is called Munchausen's syndrome by proxy. The child may be unaware that the parent is intentionally hurting him to satisfy his own need to seek comfort from a doctor.

While Munchausen's is considered self-mutilation, it is very rare. This is a life-threatening disorder of a chronic nature. Feigning illness because you don't want to go to school is not the same thing. In that circumstance, you're well aware that you aren't sick and you have a good reason why you'd like others to think you are sick.

Sufferers of Munchausen's syndrome don't simply pretend. They study various illnesses and learn how to mimic the symptoms. They don't seem to get anything out of the experience except a lot of pain and a lot of surgeries and spend most of their days and nights in hospital beds. Munchausen's syndrome is an extreme, rare form of self-mutilation.

How to Help a Friend
Who Is Self-Mutilating

Perhaps you're reading this book because you are concerned about a friend's behavior. She's grown remote and spends more time by herself instead of talking on the phone with you each night. The other day, she saw you looking at the cuts on her arm, so she wore a jacket around the rest of the day. You worried. You'd seen the fresh cuts. Later you asked her what they were. She said they were nothing. Of course, you don't believe her, but you don't know what to say. Most of all, you don't understand. If she is cutting on herself, is it a cry for help? And what are you supposed to do?

Helpful Things to Do or Say

1. If you suspect that your friend is engaging in self-mutilating behaviors, particularly if you've seen the evidence, bring up the subject. Speaking about it shows concern. Ignoring it won't make it go away.

2. It's okay to bring up your concerns as long as you don't lecture or play psychologist. If your friend denies the obvious, consider that she may not yet be ready to talk about it.

3. Read about self-inflicted violence (check the resource section at the back of this book). The more you understand, the more understanding you can be to your friend.

4. Ask questions about her life, and take the time to listen to what she says. Notice her nonverbal communication as well as her verbal so that you can better understand her feelings.

5. Say things such as, "You seem angry when you say that ...." or "You look really unhappy right now." Sometimes, people don't realize how they feel until someone else points it out to them. It's helpful to clarify how she presents herself.

6. Ask her how you can be of help. More often than not, the best thing a friend can offer is a shoulder to cry on and an ear to listen. If she has other suggestions, consider them if they sound appropriate. Each person knows best how she can be helped.

7. Spend time with your friend and really listen to her. Nonetheless, set reasonable boundaries. That means you don't have to be available to talk to her 24 hours a day, and you don't have to do her homework for her.

8. Talk to her about seeking professional help but try to keep the decision to get treatment her decision. Your job is to support.

9. If she refuses to get treatment, and you are concerned for her safety, talk to a trusted adult: her parents, your school counselor, your minister, or your own parents.

10. If at any point she threatens suicide, take the threat very seriously. Contact a trusted adult or a professional immediately.

Things Not to Do or Say

1. Once you've seen the evidence of self-mutilation, don't ignore it. By not saying anything, your friend may assume you don't care or it's not important.

2. On the other hand, don't overreact. If you act shocked or disgusted, your friend is not going to feel safe telling you how he's feeling.

3. Don't lecture or judge. You may force him to defend or deny his behavior.

4. Don't tell him to stop, either. Having read this book, you now know that the self-mutilating behavior serves a purpose: it's his way of coping with strong, negative feelings. Telling him to stop is too simplistic and too threatening.

5. Don't promise to keep his secrets from adults. He may say he'll tell his parents if you promise not to tell yours, but you won't do him any favor by keeping silent.

6. Don't play psychologist with your friend. That's a job best left to the professionals.

7. However, don't assume the professionals are the only support he needs. Continue to be his friend. Stay involved in constructive activities in which you both share an interest.

8. Don't hover over him, worrying and wondering when he might hurt himself again. Excessive concern gives the impression you think he's too fragile to survive without you.

9. Don't berate him for relapses. Slipping up is not the end of the world.

10. Don't expect him to improve in any set timeframe. Overcoming self-mutilating behavior is hard work and may take months.

Conclusion

As you can see, self-mutilating behavior occurs for a variety of reasons, some more serious than others. While some teenagers may choose to self-mutilate because they're bored or they want more status with their peers, others self-injure because they don't see any other way to deal with uncomfortable thoughts and feelings. The self-mutilator chooses to carve her boyfriend's initials in her arm rather than wear a necklace bearing his initials. The angry teenager caught between fighting parents chooses to turn that anger on himself, rather than find safer ways to manage his anger. The bingeing and purging teenager chooses to control her eating and weight because she doesn't feel able to control anything else in her life.

A small number of teenagers outgrow their self-mutilating behavior as they mature and learn better coping skills. Some stop once they've outgrown the need to sit around with their friends and get high. And some teenagers stop mutilating when it finally occurs to them that their bodies deserve better treatment.

The important thing is to recognize that help is there if you need it. You can stop self-mutilating and feeling out of control. Look at the Where to Go for Help section at the end of this book to find organizations that can help you in overcoming self-mutilation.

Glossary

anorexia An eating disorder in which a person refuses to eat enough to maintain a normal body weight.

bingeing Eating enormous quantities of food or feeling unable to refrain from eating the food you want.

bulimia An eating disorder in which a person binges and then purges to avoid weight gain.

conscious When a person is well aware of what he is thinking and doing.

dissociate When a person drifts off in his mind so that he doesn't experience what is currently happening to him.

dopamine A brain chemical that is associated with schizophrenia and psychosis when too much of it exists.

drug interaction When one medication causes a more serious reaction when taken in conjunction with another medication.

malingering Pretending to be sick in order to avoid something or gain something.

MAO An enzyme in the brain whose job is to break down the chemical serotonin.

MAO inhibitors A type of antidepressant that prevents MAO from doing its job, thus maintaining higher levels of serotonin.

Munchausen's syndrome A disorder in which a person creates symptoms of a physical illness simply to remain a patient in a hospital.

norepinephrine A brain chemical that is associated with mood and alertness.

obsessive compulsive disorder A mental disorder in which a person either experiences obssessive thoughts and/or performs compulsive behaviors in order to manage anxiety.

post-traumatic stress disorder A mental disorder in which a person has suffered from some incident that is beyond the realm of normal human experience and shows symptoms of anxiey and depression.

purging Getting rid of the food and calories one has taken in, either by vomiting or excessive use of laxatives.

schizophrenia A mental disorder characterized by disorganized thinking, hallucinations, and delusional thoughts.

serotonin A brain chemical responsible for calming people, improving memory, and modulating mood.

trauma reenactment Engaging in behavior that is reminiscent of the original trauma.

unconscious A state of mind where the person is unaware of his or her thoughts or motivations.

Where to Go for Help

In the United States

The Cutting Edge (newsletter)
P.O. Box 20819
Cleveland, Ohio 44120

SAFE (Self Abuse Finally Ends)
Alternatives Program
40 Timberline Drive
Lemont, IL 60439
(800) DONTCUT
Web site: http://www.rockcreek-hosp.com

In Canada

S.A.F.E. (Self Abuse Finally Ends)
306-241 Simcoe St.
London, Ontario
CANADA N6B 3L4
(519) 434-9473
E-mail: safe@wwdc.com
Web site: http://www.wwdc.com/safe/

Web Sites

http://www.palace.net/~llama/psych/injury.html

http://www.gURL.com

http://www.mindspring.com/~thefly/selfinjury.htm

http://www.mirror-mirror.org/selfinj.htm

For Further Reading

Alderman, Tracy. *The Scarred Soul.* Oakland, CA: New
    Harbinger Publications, Inc,. 1997.
Burns, David. *The Feeling Good Handbook.* New York:
    William Morrow & Co., 1989.
Deni, Laura. *Childhood and Teen Suicides.* Kettering, OH:
    PPI Publishing, 1983.
Favazza, Armando. *Bodies Under Siege.* 2nd edition.
    Baltimore, MD: Johns Hopkins University Press, 1996.
Friedland, Bruce. *The Encyclopedia of Health: Personality
    Disorders.* New York: Chelsea House Publishers, 1991.
Gilbert, Sara D. *Get Help.* New York: Morrow Jr. Books, 1989.
Goodman, Berney. *When the Body Speaks Its Mind.* New
    York: G.P. Putnam's Sons, 1994.
Hyde, Margaret, and Elizabeth Held. *Suicide—The Hidden
    Epidemic.* New York: Franklin Watts, 1986.
Lewis, Cynthia Copeland. *Teen Suicide.* Springfield, NJ:
    Enslow Publishers, Inc., 1994.
Miller, Dusty. *Women Who Hurt Themselves.* New York: Basic
    Books, 1994.
Simpson, Carolyn and Dwain. *Coping with Post-Traumatic
    Stress Disorder.* New York: Rosen Publishing Group, 1997.
Stoehr, Shelley. *Crosses.* New York: Delacorte Press, 1991.

Index